Hale and Hearty

Looking at Things as a Whole

Alistair J. Sinclair Ph.D.

Man - of all ages and cultures - is confronted with the solution of one and the same question; the question of how to overcome separateness, how to achieve union, how to transcend one's individual life and find at-onement.
Erich Fromm, *The Art of Loving,* (1957)

AP
Almostic

Almostic Publications
2016

Published by

Almostic Publications

Glasgow

ISBN 978-0-9574044-7-2

To Anne Sackman
for her interest in my works and her sympathy and encouragement

Other Works by
Alistair J. Sinclair

BOOKS

The Answers Lies Within Us
What is Philosophy: An Introduction
The Will to Live: A Systematic Guide to Our Reasons for Living
American Papers in Humanism and Religion
Sautonic Wisdom: What We Are Here To Do
The Promise of Dualism: An Introduction to Dualist Theory

E-BOOKS

The Future of Humanity: The Need to Believe in Humanity and its Future
Vindication: Justifying Our Existence
From Time to Eternity: An Essay on the Meaning of Time
Shakespeare on Time
Punish the Person not the Crime: A New Theory of Punishment Based on
Old Principles
Old Age, Death and the After-Life
Reforming the British Constitution
The Normal Society: And How To Get It

Contents

8. Cosmos - Developing the Holistic View

Introduction

What this book is about

What is it to be 'hale and hearty'? Can we be hale and hearty throughout our lives? This book examines this state of mind and gives some hints about how to achieve it and keep it. It is about being 'hale and hearty' in the sense of being at one with ourselves and world. We aim to achieve a wholeness within us that emanates good health and heartiness. By looking at ourselves as a whole and at humanity as a whole we can find the best way forward. The aim is to achieve integrity and inner strength by constantly interacting with all the knowledge and experience that our lives have to offer. The eight exercises outlined in this book can be helpful in that regard. These mental exercises offer different viewpoints that broaden the mind and focus it on the important things about life and living. The resultant holistic view is an antidote to the overspecialisation of science on the one hand and the unworldliness of religion on the other hand.

We all lose heart from time to time. Life's disappointments, sorrows, setbacks, illnesses can afflict us all. We know that we should buck ourselves up and carry on regardless, but how do we do that? Well, this book suggests that we can strengthen ourselves within. Its mental exercises build up our inner strength and make life more bearable and enjoyable. We become wholes through acquiring a holistic view of things.

Then again, we can easily lose our way and wonder what life is all about. We doubt whether life is really worth living. This may be because we lack the reasons for living that are needed to think our way out of this impasse. The holistic view can help here also. It helps us to integrate ourselves with the life around us. By understanding better the part that we play in this integrated wholeness, we can accommodate ourselves better to life and soldier on with better heart. The holistic exercises show that there is direction and purpose to life if we strive hard enough to find these for ourselves.

These exercises help us to see ourselves as a whole, as opposed to belittling ourselves. They help us to make something of ourselves and increase our self-confidence by self-improving exercises and by adopting roles that will broaden and deepen our thinking. Only by such self-development can we achieve any lasting happiness. The exercises are intended to help in that direction by introducing a holistic view of life and its opportunities.

Thus, being 'Hale and Hearty' here means being happy in ourselves and with ourselves. We might reach this happy state by simply switching off altogether and doing nothing but lie on a beach for the rest of our lives. But happiness is wholesomeness and not just a transitory, ecstatic feeling. It is not living for the moment but living as if we live forever. This makes us responsible not just for ourselves and others but also for life and humanity, as we are an ineluctable part of both these.

Though we are here to make the most of our lives as a whole, we must find out for ourselves just what this means. The mental exercises offer hints to this meaningfulness. They can help to build up our mental strength and achieve the wholeness of which we are all capable. This is a wholeness within ourselves and not a physical wholeness that concerns things outside us. It is about getting ourselves together to do the best we can. For example, those in the thrall of drink, drugs or some kind of obsessive behaviour have lost touch with themselves. They lack the self-control and inner development to stop themselves from doing what they really don't want to do. But the more they bridge the gap between their inner life and the outer world, the more control they can have over themselves. The holistic exercises can aid this process by encouraging their self-development and increasing their self-confidence.

Being of good heart means being wholesome within and having the bigger picture in mind. Otherwise we can spend our lives groping around without achieving anything that satisfies or fulfils us. When we lose the plot, go off the rails, get off the straight and narrow, we have lost touch with ourselves as a whole. We become immersed in our petty problems that are trivial when we see them in the wider perspective. Taking account of the whole picture gives us our best chance of understanding and appreciating our place in the wider scheme of things. It bolsters our inner security to have this in mind and to find interest and stimulation in contemplating it. Everything makes more sense from afar, "From a distance there is harmony" in the words of Bette Midler's admirable song. This book is therefore an exploration of the ways of getting ourselves together so that we become *holists.*

The holist sees things as a whole and the mental exercises outlined in this book are intended to stretch the mind in a wholesome way. Each of the eight exercises adds to the holistic point of view aimed at here. They are the bare minimum required to reach such an all-encompassing view of things. That 'bare minimum' needs to be supplemented by the individual's experiences of life. They will help the individual to better value life and humanity and make more of them than otherwise. The eight exercises are *(1) Vitality (2) Illumination (3) Morality (4) Humanism (5) Optimism (6) Science (7) Art (8) Cosmos.*

Moreover, they are intended to increase our self-understanding and help us to find out what we can do with ourselves. We extend ourselves to embrace everything about humanity and about what it is to be human. We become wiser people since wisdom consists in seeing things as a whole. Thus, the holistic view involves getting to know ourselves, seeing ourselves as a whole, improving ourselves and becoming wise people as a result. It is a sign of wisdom to appreciate the value of life and humanity. Life is glorified and humanity is elevated when we do our best to benefit both of them. Thus, it is in doing worthwhile things rather than simply believing in the religious manner that we make our mark on life and humanity.

The importance of the holistic view

Looking at things as a whole is a holistic view unique to human beings. We are the only *holistic* species on this planet, as we alone can look at things as a whole, as long as we make up our minds to do so. Other animals are too rooted in the here-and-now to see the bigger picture. They are governed by instinct and present exigencies more than we are, as we can learn by upbringing to be more than instinctive or impulsive creatures. Thus, the holistic view is not acquired by instinct; we must learn it by education and experience. The task of achieving this holistic frame of mind is addressed here.

The holistic view is incompatible with extremism of any kind. The extremist typically focuses on one view to the exclusion of all others. Anyone taking the whole view cannot regard one view to be the whole truth of the matter when its merits and demerits are seen in relation to opposing views. The holistic view combats extremism by incorporating dualism and its appreciation of opposing points of view. Extremism results from one point of view being favoured to exclusion of all opposing ones. However, dualism has the problem of discriminating or judging between these points of view. The holistic view steps outside these points of view and facilitates decisiveness as to which is to be preferred. Thus, anyone who is not holistic minded can be vulnerable to extremism. A good test of whether a person is vulnerable to an extremist mentality is to ascertain the extent of their broadmindedness and openness to alternative ways of thinking.

Neither science nor religion looks at things as a whole. They cannot give us the whole picture. Science is too specialised and religion is too otherworldly and rooted in narrow beliefs. The holistic view avoids scientific specialisation on the one hand, and religious unworldliness and credulity on the other hand. It is not specialised in that it is all-embracing and all-encompassing. It is not unworldly and credulous as it takes us into the real world to do the best that we can as individuals and make it a better place to live in and prosper. Holism gives us an informed wisdom that is ever open to continuous development in the light of further thought, experience and information. It gives substance to the practical kind of wisdom characteristic of wise men down the ages. It is therefore a philosophy to be taught and understood; it is not a religion to be preached or believed in uncritically.

From the holistic viewpoint we can ascertain the extent of our ignorance of things. We can't do anything about our lack of knowledge and understanding unless we see the full extent of our deficiencies. What we do not know can never be grasped without stepping outside ourselves and broadening our imaginations in that way.

Holism takes account of all points of view without promoting any single viewpoint as being the answer to everything. It is therefore a philosophy which involves thinking about things critically and carefully. The holist can never be a single-minded demagogue or charlatan enforcing his views on other people. He can only be a teacher and never a preacher.

Moreover, the holist view does not reduce the individual to the whole. On the contrary, it is suffused with the Autonomy Principle which states that each individual is an autonomous person capable of unique and irreplaceable development. We are all ends in ourselves and the role of society is to provide the framework in which our ends can be achieved. The holist view therefore works from the individual upwards by ensuring that each person adopts that view for their own ends and not because it is imposed from above *ex cathedra.*

The role of self-improvement

The wise person looks at the whole picture in doing worthwhile things. To know the world as a whole is to know ourselves as a whole. But we can never know enough and our education never ceases unto death. In striving to improve our knowledge and understanding we improve ourselves, and self-improvement is something we can all do for ourselves.

By improving ourselves we contribute to the future of our species. We do things better than before, and therefore have more self-confidence, treat other people better, work more efficiently, and waste less time and money. When we all work together in improving ourselves, co-operation becomes more important than competition. *Self-improvement means competing with ourselves and not with other people.* There is no use emulating other people or trying to be better than them when it does not become us as individuals. We can discover for ourselves what we are suited for. In this way, we make enemies of our own inertia and incompetence, and not of other people. Thus, there is no point in thinking that we are as good as or better than other people if we lack the self-knowledge to know that we can do better.

This ethos of co-operative self-improvement brings us together as a purposeful species as opposed to being the self-destructive species that we are too often even today. This is important because humanity must make its own future, just as life has made itself in the universe in the past and is doing so at present. No creator is required as we create our own experience of life and our happiness. We have become responsible for the future of life because we know how important it is to the natural development of the universe. The forces of the universe have complexified its contents over time, and life is the end product of that process. Life has been responsible for its own complexification by improving its means of survival by reproduction (as is shown in my book *The Promise of Dualism*). We in our turn are responsible for our inner development and for cultural progress in supporting and participating in it. We are at the apex of biological advance because we know what is happening in the universe, and that knowledge makes us responsible for ensuring the best possible use of it, both as individuals and as a species. For example, we can use that knowledge to propagate and support life on this planet and elsewhere, as well as to people the moon and life-sustaining planets.

In this way, the broader view helps us to make sense of our lives and gives them purpose and direction that they may otherwise lack. We can only do these things for ourselves alone as there are no outside sources for us to rely upon, and it is a sign of our maturity as a species that we can acknowledge that fact and carry on regardless.

Finally, we are here to do as much in society as will make our lives as fulsome and wholesome as possible. In that way, we learn new ways of thinking and being while seeing the whole picture which is constantly changing and developing. Thus, constant adaptation to realities is the key to our survival and our future prosperity. In that way, we are encouraged to exercise our wisdom on a daily basis and demonstrate our worth to ourselves and others.

The life-enhancing consequences of the holistic view

The aim of the holistic view is to promote life-enhancing frames of mind which are positive, sympathetic, inclusive and developmental:

❖ *Positive frame of mind* – This looks forward to the future with hope and optimism. It sets out deliberately to avoid being depressed, self-defeating, or self-abnegating. The exercises of Vitality, Illumination and Optimism contribute to this frame of mind.

❖ *Sympathetic frame of mind* – This refers to a sympathetic view of humanity and its diversity as opposed to a negative, self-destructive view. The Humanism exercise is particularly relevant here.

❖ *Inclusive frame of mind* – This includes all points of view by not dismissing any of them out of hand. It is therefore an open-minded view of things. The exercises of Science, Art and Cosmos give us reasons to venerate and exultate all that is worthy of us as human beings.

❖ *Developmental frame of mind* – This refers to personal, intellectual, social and universal development.

Personal Development: Developing oneself personally is clearly preferable to degrading oneself with excessive, irrational and pointless behaviour. Such a development requires self-discipline and self-knowledge, whereas self-degradation results from lack of moral sense and self-criticism, as outlined in the Morality exercise.

Intellectual Development: Developing one's intellect requires critical thinking. By increasing one's knowledge and understanding by means of the exercises of Science and Art, It is not just being clever but being known to be knowledgeable and *au fait* with current affairs.

Social Development: Becoming a socially integrated and well-adjusted individual follows from a wide understanding of society and one's place in it. The Humanism exercise is particularly designed to encourage this development.

Universal Development: Developing oneself universally means putting oneself into the widest and broadest possible context. This is the particular aim of the Cosmos exercise which embodies everything that is universally worthy of us as human beings.

Thus, all the holistic exercises contribute to this frame of mind and particularly the Vitality, Illumination and Morality exercises.

The role of the holistic exercises

Holistic Wisdom is basically common sense wisdom made plain and explicit in relation to the complex knowledge and understanding now at our disposal. In so far as this wisdom can be taught, it consists in the Holistic Exercises already mentioned, namely, *(1) Vitality (2) Illumination (3) Morality (4) Humanism (5) Optimism (6) Science (7) Art (8) Cosmos*. If we lack the will to become wise then the first exercise of *Vitality* is a way of building the will within to do what needs to be done. What is within us must be brought out by *Illumination* and disciplined by *Morality* so that it can become a *Humanism* that is of service to humanity. Belief in humanity's future does not come naturally as it requires a state of mind of *Optimism*. It can be justified by contemplation of our central position in the universe which *Science* shows us that we exist between the very small and very large aspects of the universe. *Art* is about our creativity and the potential everlastingness of our creative products. Ultimately, everything that we do and think can take their place in the *Cosmos*, which expresses the holistic view that embraces every aspect of humanity and its achievements. In this way, the Holistic Exercises fit together and give a comprehensive view of what we are and what we can achieve as individuals and as a species. The eight Holistic Exercises are also ways of vindicating ourselves in developing and exercising our intelligence and creativity. They lead to our performing the roles that are outlined as follows:

Social Exercises – establishing one's role in society

(1) **Vitality** – *Vitalist* – living intensely – essential to inner growth

(2) **Illumination** – *Illuminist* – enlightening the world – making for cheerfulness

(3) **Morality** – *Moralist* – behaving well – enabling us to be at one with ourselves and others

(4) **Humanism** – *Humanist* – serving humanity – making us useful and obliging citizens

Universal Exercises – establishing one's place in the universe

(5) **Belief** – *Optimist* – believing in life and humanity – essential for our future

(6) **Science** – *Scientist* – understanding the material universe – making sense of science

(7) **Art** – *Artist* – bringing new creations into being – giving a place for art

(8) **Cosmos** – *Holist* – getting in touch with everything – bringing humanity to the fore

The first four of these concern our place in society and therefore social self-development. The second four deal with our place in the universe and therefore with universal self-development.

In summary, therefore, these exercises are essential tools in attaining Holistic Wisdom. They aim to increase our self-knowledge, promote inner development, strengthen our character and integrity and make us better and more productive individuals. By their means, we become familiar with a wide range of social roles and these help us to appreciate the diversity and complexity of humanity.

The role of role play

In performing the various exercises, we adopt the roles implied by them. These help us to improve ourselves holistically. The roles given here are as follows: (1) Vitalist, (2) Illuminist, (3) Moralist, (4) Humanist, (5) Optimist, (6) Scientist, (7) Artist, and (8) Holist. These roles are not intended to be exhaustive of the possibilities. They are only those that may be sufficient in themselves to make a difference and take us to higher plains of existence than hitherto possible.

How these roles work out in practice is summarised as follows:-

Vitalist – has inner strength that enables them to see significance even in a humdrum work-a-day existence. Building up inner being to enhance vitality is not only fundamental to the acquisition of wisdom but also to the control and modulation of intuitive thinking.

Illuminist – wants to combat negativity with the light of knowledge and understanding. Only by pouring greater light on things can we expect clarity and get inspiration.

Moralist – possesses the strength of purpose to do the right thing that benefits other people as much as themselves.

Humanist – sees serving others as a vital form of self-expression. We are less than human unless we make ourselves useful to others.

Optimist – is optimistic about the future of humanity provided it makes the necessary effort to ensure and enhance its future. The true optimist does not give up, not ever.

Scientist – explores the middle ground and is perennially curious and looks to understand more and more about the universe. By that means we expand our understanding and our view of our role in it.

Artist – is creative and wishes to make a lasting mark on the world. The artist is ecstatic about life and its opportunities and wishes to adopt an eternal point of view which is the essence of being artistic in ways that have eternal resonances.

Holist – takes account of human achievements as a whole and sees their value in making for an all-inclusive Cosmos.

Each role plays its part in helping us to develop (1) our inner strength as *Vitalists*, (2) our ability to shine forth as *Illuminists,* (3) our moral discipline as *Moralists*, (4) our usefulness to others as *Humanists*, (5) our belief in humanity and its future as *Optimists*, (6) our scientific outlook as *Scientists*, (7) our intuitive creativity as *Artists*, and (8) our breadth of understanding as *Holists* These can help us vindicate our existence on this planet and save ourselves from our own inconsequentiality.

The holistic idea is that by exercising the above roles, we can make (1) the most of ourselves to the limits of our abilities, (2) grasp the whole meaning and truth of humanity, and (3) see everything as a whole and no longer in terms of one single point of view. Learning about these roles is a matter of education and not indoctrination. We can all learn about them though we need not be equally interested in them all. There is no compulsion involved as we can follow our natural bent and make our own use of the eight roles in pursuing our interests.

The various roles are complementary in that they all contribute to our whole being. As Vitalists we bring out what is within us; as Illuminists we enlighten ourselves and others; as Moralists we discipline ourselves to do our best to the best of our abilities; as Humanists we serve other people to the benefit of all humanity; as Optimists we have confidence in humanity's future and wish to contribute to it; as Scientists in the broadest sense we seek understanding of everything around us and of our place in the universe; as Artists we express our creativity and eternalise all our thoughts and deeds in preparation for their being left behind us for future generations and posterity in general; and as Holists we organise our knowledge in relation to the Cosmos as a whole and make our overall contribution to the repository of the Cosmos. There is also a universality about these roles that is outlined here:

Basic Role	*Universal Role*	*Its Universality*
Vitalist	Internalist	The vitalist is also an internalist by invoking the internal life of subjectivity and making the most of it.
Illuminist	Externalist	The illuminist shines forth by virtue of what is within him and therefore externalises his inner life for the benefit of others.
Moralist	Normalist	The moralist is a normalist who advocates adhesion to the norms of society to maximise freedom with responsibility.
Humanist	Socialist/ Capitalist	In serving others we benefit society and can perform the dual roles of socialists and capitalists by combining these views and avoiding the extremes implied by them.
Optimist	Protagonist	The protagonist is essentially optimistic because of the strength of his beliefs about humanity's future.
Scientist	Centralist	The centralist is also a scientist in that scientific knowledge extends from the centre towards the very small and very large things in the universe.
Artist	Eternalist	The eternalist sees the biggest possible picture and in his actions becomes an artist contributing to posterity and the eternity that lies beyond it.
Holist	Cosmist	The Cosmos is the repository of order so that the cosmist is also a harmonist in seeking to harmonise the chaos surrounding us.

Holism and Science

Holism embodies the scientific outlook in so far as that outlook is a part of our natural way of thinking. Each of the roles covers some aspect of that outlook.

- Our vitality reflects the enthusiasm that scientific ideas can give us about life. We make science part of not just our objective view of the world but also of our subjective as it becomes part of what we are when we view the world.

- In illuminating life, we shed light on things. Such illumination involves also the light that science can pour on our lives. The universe shines for us in all its glory and complexity when we adopt the scientific view of it.
- By disciplining ourselves we learn the discipline and moral discrimination that scientific and creative endeavour requires to reach truths that benefit us all. A moral backbone is indispensable to getting things done that are valuable and worthwhile. Morality also gives us the conceptual skills required to distinguish what is valuable and worthwhile from what is not.
- Believing in our future is characteristic of the scientific view and it fuels their endeavours. Scientists are implicitly if not explicitly contributing to our future and therefore they must harbour some belief in it.
- Serving humanity includes the service that science renders to society by making our lives better and more comfortable materially.
- The middle ground is the perspective from which all science is conducted. It is therefore augmented by our scientific advances so that we gain knowledge both macroscopically and microscopically and about everything else within these extremes.
- The eternal nature of artistic achievement includes also the creativity and beauty of scientific knowledge as well as the fact that it gives us eternal truths about ourselves and the universe.
- We contribute to the Cosmos with the order and beauty of our knowledge and creative endeavours. The Cosmos goes beyond the material universe to incorporate what humanity has contributed through its intelligence and creativity of which science is the mainstay.

Holism and Religion

Religion, as a single answer, is no longer right for us as we have now gone beyond it in our cultural development. Religion has been part of our cultural development but it is no longer the ultimate answer on which to base the future of our culture. The Bible and other sacred scriptures give us insights into the human condition but they are no longer relevant to modern culture. They do not contain absolute truths that we can rely on to the exclusion of other sources of truth. For example, we can now be certain that the biblical Garden of Eden story is not just an allegorical story it also gives us a completely mistaken view of our origins. Our knowledge of the past now tells us that there was no previous state of innocence from which we were corrupted by knowledge of good and evil. There was no 'original sin' committed by Adam and Eve that plagues us all. The evidence afforded by studying animals, primitive tribes, the archaeology of early man and similar knowledge tells us that there was no state of nature that was totally pure and innocent. In fact, it was by learning to distinguish between good and evil behaviour that we learned to be moral beings. We are only really human when we exercise moral restraint and do not simply do what we feel like doing. We punish ourselves and wrong each other when we fail to restrain ourselves in the certain knowledge that we could have done better. We don't need holy scripture to teach us such things as it is natural for us to behave thus when we are being true to ourselves.

The holistic view teaches us that we must rely on ourselves to save us. Religion may claim to save people through faith, obedience or restraint, but it is too often used by charlatans to assert power and authority over people by such claims or by offering doctrines that 'save' them in some way. But we must save ourselves together as a unified species. Our future is in our own hands because there is nothing else for it. In humanism, humanity takes responsibility for itself. Instead of crying out 'God save us!' or 'God wills it!' in any predicament, we must ask what we can do to save ourselves. This is our role as humanists and optimists, as is argued in more detail below in the relevant sections. We have to make our own future, even if we may do so ineffectively or haphazardly, for we have always benefited more from a trial-and-error process in progressing than from the imposition of authoritarian doctrines. Thus, the holist view is optimistic about our future without believing that our future is secure. We must do what we can to ensure that future and to make it better place for our descendants. Briefly, there is no future in God as it harks back to our past.

This is therefore a humanist philosophy that takes account of all religions, but it nevertheless has its limitations. It is not 'all things to all men' as it is limited in its scope and content. For example, it is intolerant of unnecessary extremes. It does not condone the transformation of human beings by genetic engineering unless it is to cure disease or disability. We must work within both our genetic inheritance and the environment that is given to us. We are not necessarily any better for making life any easier than it already is, since the ultimate enjoyment lies in overcoming difficulties and by facing challenges instead of shunning them.

Holism and Humanism

More than any religion, humanism tolerates differences between human beings, perhaps to a fault. A 'live and let live' policy is the very essence of the humanist outlook. 'Bear and forbear' – this includes the inner strength of putting up with people's annoying behaviour for the sake of peace and harmony. The truly strong man is he who resists and desists in the face of provocation and annoyance, and can forbear from reacting to these. In that regard, humanism has taken on the Christian repudiation of vengeance and of reacting to provocation. It consists in turning the other cheek, loving one's enemies and not judging others.

There are however limits to which differences can be tolerated. There may be a need sometimes to be intolerant of intolerance. Those who are intolerant of other people's beliefs do not deserve to be tolerated by society. 'To live and let live' is a fine maxim for religious and political toleration in general. It preaches that we should carry on with our lives without worrying about people who live and think differently from ourselves. But it would be unwise to apply it when one is confronted with a homicidal maniac who wishes to kill people. There are limits to its application. When one sector of society is absolutely intolerant of the rest of society and wishes to impose its culture on the rest of society then the limits of toleration are surely reached, and the cancerous growth of that antipathetic sector may call for suppression for the sake of society's general health and harmony.

The holist view takes in the whole human race and therefore abhors racism that divides people irrationally. Thus, human racism is the only admissible form of racism. As human racists we function at our best between the extremes of belief and scepticism and between the extremes of (1) believing human beings to be nothing but animals and (2) believing them to be in the image of God. This can be represented as follows:

Belief

↕

Animals ↔ *THE HUMAN RACIST* ↔ Gods

↕

Scepticism

Both the godly and animalist extremes lessen us as human beings. The one subordinates us to ideas or creeds of some sort. The other becomes an excuse for doing nothing at all as all beliefs can be reduced to nothing by verbal reasoning and over reliance on words and arguments. We are more than just animals by the fact that we can differentiate ourselves from them in our behaviour and in our feelings. But at the same time we make ourselves in our own image and we need no imaginary entity to look up to and demean ourselves thereby.

Those who have more regard for animals than for human beings might as well live with animals as they are apparently unsuited to be living among us. Those who put God before humanity are similarly unsuited to human society since we can never live up to the standards and demands of a god hanging over us. The godly view is dogmatically restrictive and the animalist view is sceptically indefinite. The holistic view rejects the extremes of absolute dogmatic belief on the one hand and of insipid scepticism on the other hand. Thus, it is at the middle of things that we constantly have the problem of what it is to be a human being and it is at the centre that we must find our answers, as is implied by the scientific, centralist view dealt with below.

Holism as a philosophy

The holistic view is a philosophy or way of life by which we can achieve a greater self-awareness concerning our role in society and our place in the universe, thus arriving at a better understanding of what to do with our lives. It is a special sort of wisdom that promotes sufficient inner development to achieve self-knowledge regarding one's relationship to society and the universe. It shows how all our personal, social and universal aims can be reconciled. Whatever we do for ourselves ought *ipse facto* to be good for life and humanity. If it is not good in that way then we have gone wrong into our thinking and doing. The holistic view therefore provides the tools by which each individual can find out for themselves what is the right way of thinking and doing for them. It is not imposed on the individual but offered as an educational way forward rather than a doctrinal one. It is something to think about and is not intended to be the ultimate answer but a way to get at the best available answers given the knowledge available to us at this point in time. It is designed to promote further thought and not bring thinking to an end.

Knowledge consists in knowing what to do and how and where to do it; wisdom consists in knowing if it is worth doing and when best to do it. Thus, knowing what or how to do things is not enough. The wisdom is also needed to stand above the said knowledge and to use it wisely. Wisdom gives us the effective strategy we need to make the best possible use of our knowledge. Moreover, wisdom is not just an end in itself, it also has the goal of attaining ultimate truth in the full knowledge that it never can be reached. Thus, *The Ultimacy Principle* implies the following:

> *You can't know truth without considering the possibility of ultimate truth that includes everything about life, humanity and the universe.*

In striving for the elusive and unattainable goal of ultimate truth we incorporate all human achievements and all the possibilities lying before us in the future. This makes *cosmic holists* out of us. This *Ultimacy Principle* is something to strive for over and above ourselves, and Holism at least points the way. This means that the ultimate ambition of the holist is to take account of everything concerning life and the human race, and the holistic roles offer a way to achieve this. This seems to be the best way to improve ourselves and contribute to the betterment of life and humanity.

The basic message of holism is that we are here to exploit our vitality, illuminate life, discipline ourselves, serve humanity, believe in our future, expand the middle ground, embrace eternity, and contribute to the Cosmos. If we can do all that, we may expect no better of life. Working out the meaning of our existence and our place in the universe is an important part of holism. Such holistic roles may therefore be helpful in finding a solution to the problem of existence provided they are properly learnt and effectively put into practice. Moreover, they are instruments of exploration intended to stimulate further thought. They are not definitive but provisional, and are a beginning rather than an end. If a person is no better for working through them then they are to no avail. There are two further holistic principles which are *The Social Principle* and *The Universal Principle* as follows:

(1) You can't know yourself properly without understanding your place in society;

(2) You can't know society properly without understanding humanity's place in the universe.

Firstly, as social animals we function at our best in a social environment. If we are entirely divorced from the company of other people we cannot develop or function properly as human personalities. Thus the first of these principles is essential for *Social Self-Development*. It makes use of the first four of the roles of the Vitalist, Illuminist, Moralist and Humanist, in so far as these contribute to our self-development.

Secondly, human society only makes sense within the context of the universe as a whole. Our complex society is the latest of the complex entities that have evolved in the universe. The more we understand how our society fits into the universe, the more we are comfortable with the roles we play in it. (Such understanding is reinforced by dualist theory as outlined in my book, *The Promise of Dualism*). Thus, our importance as a species results from our understanding more than any other animal on the planet what we are and are not in the universe. Our self-confidence as individuals may be boosted by thinking of ourselves in the widest possible context, namely, the universe as a whole. In short, our self-knowledge is incomplete if it does not include this universal component. This principle promotes *Universal Self-Development* and makes use of the second four roles concerning the Optimist, Scientist, Artist and Holist to maintain our self-development. These roles are intended to supply the broadest possible view of humanity and how we relate to the universe as a whole.

There are reciprocal interrelationships between all these roles that are potentially never-ending and are dualist in nature. The holistic view embodies these interrelationships Continuous self-improvement from one day to the next may be boosted when there is a cyclical repetition of these interrelationships. Static and unresponsive personalities no longer participate in this unending cycle of growing self-knowledge. This therefore describes what we do when we are being active beings who are constantly relating to our surroundings, other people and society at large. Thus, holism is about the activity of getting worthwhile things done as opposed to the passivity of accepting things just as they are.

In practical terms, the holistic view aims to bring the whole of life and humanity into one's self. One becomes at one with the world, the universe and ultimately the Cosmos. This is an atonement or at-one-ment that everyone can seek and achieve by making the most of their lives. Religions such as Buddhism find that atonement in being, but the holistic view is about doing rather than being. One must ever strive to achieve and maintain atonement. Being at one with the world means living not just for one's own selfish purposes but also for the purposes of life and humanity. This view brings these two aspects together so that we are always striving to reconcile our selfish and altruistic propensities. In this way, the doing of holism replaces the being of religion.

We are not meant to live entirely for ourselves alone and we not meant to live entirely for others to whom we devote our lives selflessly. We can live for one and all. We need both solitude and society if we want to be well-rounded individuals with fully fulfilled lives. An interaction between these aspects of our nature enables us to achieve seek a healthy balance between them. Firstly, through self-expression we can add to the diversity of humanity and, secondly, through self-sacrifice we can contribute to the harmony and unity of humanity. Both of these are needed to ensure that we all contribute to the balanced progress of humanity. We live to benefit everyone; and everyone lives to benefit the single individual – "All for one and one for all". But we need to be unified by common aims and purposes to achieve this interactive balance between one and all. The holistic view shows the complexities involved in maintaining such a balanced way of living.

1. Vitality - Building Ourselves Up

A. The Need to Develop Ourselves Within

We start off our quest for wholeness by building up our mental strength within. This means increasing our vitality and becoming vitalists who are full of the vibrancy of life and living. Such vitality comprises the za-zoom, the extra energy required to get worthwhile things done. We cannot be wise persons without having something special within us that makes us want to continue living and doing things. This special ingredient gives us the *raison d'être* to do what needs to be done in asserting ourselves on the world. It gets us out of our beds and gets us going in the mornings. Without this extra chutzpah, here called vitality, we are meek and humble beings awaiting our fate without doing anything about it. This additional involvement within us is produced by what is here called 'inner being'. It is extra and additional but it is still entirely physical. There is nothing occult or supernatural about inner being as herein conceived. It is however that which makes us complicated beings instead of being straightforwardly predictable like machines or simple organisms. It also gives us the edge over the internet that lacks the centrality to make it a distinctive entity. Whether it will ever achieve that centrality or 'singularity' remains to be seen.

Self-knowledge involves knowing what one is capable of and what underlies that capability. Thus, a better understanding of the source of our vitality, namely, inner being is essentially to self-knowledge. This 'inner being' is entirely material and yet highly complex and unfathomable. Getting in touch with our inner being involves examining ourselves and what we do with ourselves. This is a circular self-reflection that is an art rather than a science. It cannot be taught but must be achieved by each of us on our own. If a person cannot sit in a room on their own and quietly get in touch with their thoughts, they will find it difficult to become vitalists in the sense of the word used here. It means being in touch with that which is within us. If we are absorbed or pre-occupied with what lies without us, getting in touch with our inner being may prove difficult and challenging.

Clearly, vitality is the essence of life and the mainspring of our existence. Without vitality of some sort we cannot motive ourselves to do anything let alone do the best we can. It is the unifying force within us that gets us going and keeps us going throughout life. It is the 'all' within us that makes us at 'one' with ourselves. We need to build it up and keep it working for us otherwise we lose our way and become depressed, obsessed, over-anxious, suicidal, anti-social or just plain bored with life. By understanding our vitality we can rally it within ourselves. When we understand it sufficiently to make something of it, we become vitalists. We have to invoke the vitality within us by whatever means. Understanding vitality thus means entering a sphere of self-knowledge within which we can better understand ourselves and our capabilities.

We need to work hard to make the most of our vitality. It is by developing our inner being that we can become a vital force instead of weak and vacillating individuals that do little or nothing with our lives. Therein we invoke what is alive and vital within us and become vitalists in the best sense of the word. Without the requisite vitality we have nothing in us to make us do anything of any lasting value. Invoking what is in us enable us to surpass ourselves and do more that we thought we could do. We use our intelligence and creativity both to develop our inner being and to do things in the world. The interaction between these two inner and outer aspects is what makes us vital beings. As vitalists we can bring out our intelligence and creativity in the service of humanity. It is a matter of putting ourselves constantly to the test in understanding our inner workings.

Bringing out the best in us consists in exploiting the potential which lies within us. What is within us is our inner being which comprises the subjective, mental activity that is peculiar to each and every one of us. It includes consciousness, self-consciousness as well unconscious mental activity. It is often inaccurately called 'spirit', 'vital energy', 'universal mind', or whatever. But these terms are misleading as they suggest something non-material whereas inner being can be explained entirely in physical terms.

Invoking our inner being is arguably the best way to integrate the perfectionist and fallibilist tendencies in our thinking about things. Such an invocation takes the mind to higher planes of existence within which such tendencies may be related and brought together in terms of the best goals and purposes to which the individual is capable of aspiring. We invoke our inner being whenever we do things that conform to the needs and aspirations of our whole personality. Such an invocation is a holistic activity that unifies us in our most prized endeavours so that we do indeed do what is best for us, given all the information at our disposal.

Moreover, it is the practical use of inner being that is being emphasised here. When we successfully invoke our inner being, we are ready to use it actively in a social context. Inner being is such that it must be constantly activated so that it might not stagnate and deteriorate into apathy, dogmatism and extremism. Firstly, we must examine what inner being consists in. Secondly, we consider what kind of training can help us to develop and bring out the best within us. This includes the exercises in the book as well as the capacity to introspect. We cannot underestimate the extent to which introspection and solitude are important in cultivating inner being. However, it must be remembered that vitality invokes our subjective dispositions to do things, and these dispositions or feelings do not always conform to reality. They must be constantly monitored and subjected to interactive examination and discrimination to weed out what is false and harmful to us. Constant self-criticism is ever needed to keep us on the straight and narrow.

B. The Vitality of our Inner Being

What 'inner being' is all about. There is a unified activity within us that makes us what we are and that forms the basis of our vitality. It is here called 'inner being' as opposed to 'outer being' which is our physical body as it is perceived by us from outside us. Inner being is what is going on inside our bodies that cannot be perceived directly, though it nevertheless exists physically. It makes the difference being alive and being dead. As human beings we have various names for different aspects of inner being, such as consciousness, self, ego, 'I', subjectivity, personality, will, character and all the names we use to refer to our distinctiveness and uniqueness as living beings. But inner being also includes all the unconscious mental activity that is always going in the brain. It is not to be confused with simplistic terms such as 'spirit' and 'soul' that have theological connotations. Inner being has a purely material basis in the body and is not distinct from the physical processes going on in the body. All living beings have an inner being that makes them distinctive as life-forms as opposed to mere lumps of matter.

The term 'inner being' is used here in two senses. It is used as a self-referential notion to refer to ourselves and what we do introspectively, and it is also used to refer objectively to what is going on in our bodies that unifies our bodily activity and makes us distinctive as living beings. In the latter sense, inner being is embedded in our bodies and is not distinct from the workings of our bodies. It is identical to what is going on in our brains and in our central and peripheral nervous systems. At death, it perishes with the rest of the body of which it is an integral part during our life-times. It may be described as a strange attractor in the body that loses its centrality, so that dissolution and disorder ensues. Inner being is thus rooted in material reality and it results from the biological and metabolic interactions occurring in our bodies. Its nature is both ideal and real in that it is an interactive link between these two contexts. The conscious part of inner being results from a self-reference process in which the strange attractor turns into itself to make self-awareness possible. This gives rise to the introspective use of the 'inner being' and this aspect is now discussed.

Inner being includes the unconscious processes that link us to reality on an ongoing basis while we are awake even though we are unaware of them. We are embedded in reality and relate to it by the workings of our inner being which interacts with what is given in reality through our senses and the conceptions we arrive at concerning the content that reality. We see the clouds in the sky but we are only aware of them as being clouds because we have arrived at conceptions of clouds based on our understanding of what we see. That understanding itself results from unconscious processes that relate our conception of clouds to what we see. These processes form part of our inner being that works hard constantly to incorporate such knowledge. The initiative to understand anything therefore depends on our adapting and developing inner being to arrive at such an understanding.

Inner being also governs the strength or weakness of our so-called 'character'. Generally speaking, the stronger our character, the more developed is our inner being. Its development is the *sine qua non* of a vital and affirmative attitude to life. Sustaining this development enables us to keep going against all the odds. It is the source of all will-power and self-determination and it develops over time through an intensification and unification of our experiences of life. It therefore forms the basis of one's personality, namely, that which is unique and singular about us.

This inner development bolsters our resolve to value our lives. Not thinking well of ourselves, as having some value and importance in the world, impairs our ability to improve ourselves and benefit other people to the best of our abilities. A developed inner being concentrates our thoughts and feelings and renders them more intense. As a result we can relate more holistically and completely with our experiences and make more of them. We get more pleasure and satisfaction from our daily experiences and value them and are more pleased with ourselves as a result.

The unified nature of inner being also gives us our conscience whereby we monitor our behaviour and adjust it accordingly in so far as we pay attention to the dictates of conscience. It is the intuition that holds us back when, for example, we feel that we are going too far or are making too much of a situation. Psychopaths and sociopaths typically have lost touch with their inner being and have no conscience. They feel no remorse, shame or guilt for their misdeeds. Their feelings are dislocated from the consequences of their actions. They are not complete personalities because of this disability and are less than human in their lack of feelings.

Inner being involves constant internal interaction between unconscious influences. It is sustained by physical processes within us that underlie the unconscious workings of our minds. It encompasses (1) the genetic influences given to us from our original conception onwards, (2) the build up of habits and routines in the process of our personality development, and (3) the intuitions, impulses, habits, routines and immediate experiences generated by that inner being below the level of consciousness. These three influences intermingle and interact to maintain the dynamism of inner being which never can be pinned down as being one thing or another.

The strength of inner being may be exemplified as follows: On a fine summer's day, I am lying idly outside in the sun when there is gardening to be done. Unless I am inwardly moved in some way, I can't be bothered doing anything. Perhaps I am in need of the rest. But merely being lazy is no excuse and my conscience may prick me. In that case, the strength of my inner being is needed to make the difference between feeling the need to do some gardening and not being bothered to do it. I must feel moved to do it. An aspect of my self becomes differentiated as a positive force in my inner being. It is I alone who must do this and nothing else will do it. The negativity of my inner passivity is countered by its positive aspects which generate further thoughts and feelings on the matter. I need to do this for such and such reasons.

If the need to do gardening is to overcome my negative feelings of laziness and indifference, I must think about what is or is not to be done to accomplish this self-imposed task. Nothing will be achieved if I think of someone else doing it or think too much of the effort involved in doing it. In thinking positively of myself doing this gardening, I am consciously focusing on the task and I can then summon up the will to do them. In the end, the power of a unified inner being is needed to ensure that any negative feelings to the contrary are suppressed and that I am consciously disposed to act as I should. In this way, I am interacting with the positive and negative inclinations of my inner being to get myself to do things. And there is no distinction between my doing the task and my inner being impelling me to do it since they are ultimately at one on the matter when I actually do what I intend to do. We can have all the motivation in the world but unless we have the will to do it, nothing can make us do what should be done. The inner being is the sole source of that will power.

While inner being is a physical activity, it is also more than the sum of its components. The physical processes by themselves alone cannot give us our experience of a supervened subjectivity that defines what we are. The activity of these processes acting purposefully and in unison is required to supervene the components of inner being. We are aware that this supervention takes place only because we have non-reducible, subjective experiences that are over and above the underlying physical processes. Reductionists reduce inner being to its basic physical components and say that there is nothing above or beyond these components. They assume that as inner being cannot be pointed to or excised by surgery, therefore it cannot exist in reality. But they are 'nothing butterists' who cannot see the wood for the trees. The fact is that we are not composed of nothing but matter and energy, nor are we determined only by our genetic inheritance, nor are we impelled by nothing but physical and chemical activity. We are more than all these things otherwise we would be indistinguishable from non-organic entities such as stones, liquids and gases. But it is only the complexity of unified physical activity in the brain that is responsible for inner being and not any additional spiritual component.

Ultimately, it is our purposefulness that is the source of our vitality. In pursuing our purposes, we unify our inner resources to get things done. Such purposes are not entirely predictable or calculable. Indeed, it is a truism that life is not entirely mechanical or automatic in its functioning. A living organism is not a machine but a teleological being capable of changing its inner configurations in relation to its goals and purposes. It is composed of cells and organs, each of which functions purposefully in relation to the whole entity. Neither the whole nor its parts operate automatically or algorithmically in the way that a computer operates. They operate by a flexible feedback with their environment that involves reacting to information received. These reactions are not wholly predictable and they give rise to goals, functions and other modes of purposeful activity peculiar to living beings. What happens inside them is unlike what happens in purely material entities that lack the attribute of life. Thus, inner being involves the purposeful, unified activity of the body, while being indistinguishable from that body and its physical components at the level of physical examination. It is at the higher level of unified, complex interactions that inner being becomes distinguishable.

Furthermore, a unified inner being is essential to the continuance of life. In general terms, biological entities are characterised by unified internal activity which is distinct from their external environment while interacting with that environment at the same time. When that unified internal activity ceases, these entities die. They are no longer living organisms but inert lumps of matter. Something has changed within them that they need to keep them alive and functional. It is their unified inner being that has ceased to function so that the body begins to fall apart. The inner being functions as the goal-making activity that unifies the organism and keeps it going against the odds. Life begins as bundles of cells that have no distinct organs but they have unifying activity that keeps them together. Thus, the unifying activity is not centred on any particular organ but on the whole body acting as an interactive unity. The various organs develop while being connected to the overall unity of the body. The stopping of the heart does not necessarily mean that death follows. Its function can be taken over by a heart-lung machine. The heart itself cannot work properly without the support and input of other major organs such as the brain, liver and kidneys. It does not orchestrate the functioning of all these organs since that functioning requires the impetus of inner being to sustain its activity. That is to say, the heart depends on the unconscious functioning of nervous activity that stimulates it to beat rhythmically according to the needs of the whole organism. It also depends on the food and oxygen supplied again by the whole organism in its unified functioning.

Our inner harmony also requires unifying processes. Inner being is required to harmonise the functioning of bodily organisms and it does so by means of its goals, both conscious and unconscious. In being the organising principle, that ensures the continued life of an organism, inner being harmonises all the processes and organs whose combined functioning is required to keep the organism alive and kicking. It unifies the organism in relation to its goals, aims, desires and aspirations, and in its turn it is produced by that unity and maintains the unity. Hence its activity interacts with all bodily functions in maintaining that unity. It is initiated and sustained by the feedback activity of the goals which the whole organism has in common from its genetic inheritance. It is not an identifiable thing or substance but the unified processes of the body in themselves. On the one hand, inner being is an interactive, self-referential notion that has no fixed essence of its own. On the other hand, it refers to that ever-flowing process which unifies all physical and metabolic processes within us and supplies all the feelings, intuitions and thoughts that constantly beset us. Much of the activity of inner being takes place in our unconscious to which we have only limited access. Thus, the different organs of the body function directly in response to processes governed by the unified inner being working at an unconscious level. They may function at their own pace and within their own limits but their activity also depends on communication with all the other organs to work in harmony with them.

The unified activity of inner being is therefore necessary for the maintenance of life. A comatose person remains alive because of the continued metabolic activity in brain and body. This is the same as saying that inner being is keeping them alive. Death comes when the failure of vital organs such as the heart, liver and brain destroys the unified functioning of the body thus stopping the inner being's activity. Inner being depends on these organs as much as they depend on it to keep them working in harmony. As inner being does not survive death, it is not anything like the soul which is believed by religious people to survive death. Only the effects of inner activity during our lifetime outlive us in the form of our works and our influences on others. It is these vital effects that we need to make the most off in developing our inner being so that we make our mark on the world during our lifetimes, and not during some mythical, non-existent afterlife.

It is also apparent that inner being cannot be replicated in another body. It is fundamentally unique to each of us and is a biological phenomenon which only comes into being within the medium of a biological entity. It cannot be reproduced independently of the entity in which it is rooted as it forms the unique being of that entity. Inner being is interconnected with the entire body and it is indivisible and cannot be reconstituted by copying the body down to the last atom and molecule. Such a replicated body would have no consciousness or sense of self since it would lack the unifying quality of the original unified activity of inner being. That unifying quality is arguably rooted at the quantum level of existence, and until we can manipulate quantum particles, we will not replicate living beings merely by reconstructing their atomic and molecular structure in the same way. That quantum activity is itself linked to the workings of the universe as whole. It cannot be taken away from us without changing the universe as whole. The evidence supporting this quantum view lies in the freewill by which we decide to do or not to do things. This can only have its source in the indeterminacy of quantum functioning and this occurs at the very smallest level at which inner being unifies bodily functions and achieves physical acts such as raising one's arm. The decision to raise one's arm therefore requires quantum activity that ultimately percolates through the entire body and involves both the brain and central and peripheral nervous systems.

These arguments suggest that there is no possibility of transporting inner being to another body because the unified operation of that particular body involves inaccessible quantum activity. Thus, the functioning of inner being is unique to each individual and cannot be recreated in another brain or body. As already stated, in the absence of inner being, the body falls into disunity, and inner being has no existence outside the body of which it is an inextricable part. They are seamlessly combined into an irreducible whole. The proof of this lies in the reality of the inner being's activity which is in no particular place in the body. We are all stuck with an inner activity that is unique to ourselves and cannot be transported elsewhere since what we are is inextricably bound up with our bodies in ways that may ultimately defeat the attempts of the most intricate technology to disentangle it.

2. Illumination - Enlightening Everything

A. Illuminating the Darkness Within

The contrast between the vitalist and the illuminist is that of being introverted and extraverted. The one is an internalist and the other an externalist. The internalist within us needs to be brought out into the light to become a more balanced personality. The development of inner being is to no avail if it does not switch on a light within us that can be used to illuminate the world. It is moving ourselves forward into the light and bringing our inner life out into the light. Thus, illumination is an important starting point for making ourselves fit for the world. We can get too wrapped up in our thoughts and feelings. Our dark side can emerge all too easily and fill us with despair. For lurking in inner being is the darkness of the soul. Thus, we need to pour light on this darkness and dispel it. Illumination is required to counter excessive introspection and bring us into the light of love and understanding. We need to bring out what is within us so that others can see our inner worth. Otherwise we remain stunted introverts having nothing to say or do with ourselves. Thus, illumination is the antidote to excessive obsession with self. It is the externality that contrasts with the internality in which the vitalist can become too involved.

The purpose of illumination is to pour light on our lives and enable us to see them more acutely and accurately than before. The illuminist therefore takes pride in shining a light on life. Light is after all the mainstay of the universe which came into being with a blaze of light that is still with us to this day. Shining a light on things means looking on the bright side of life. It makes us cheerful and optimistic so that our company is a delight to others. When brought into the light, everything makes more sense and is more endurable than otherwise. The illuminist therefore aspires to enlighten everything and everyone with the light of knowledge and understanding. This is the context in which we learn to like what we see in ourselves so that others can also like what they see in us.

Enlightening others and the world. Everyone on the planet is weighed down with their   problems, cares and worries. We can do something to ameliorate their discomforts by leading them out of the darkness with our enlightened behaviour. We behave as a worthy example to others and show them the strength of conviction that lies within us. We can all be lighthouses shedding a steady and reliable beam of light all around us. With our inner strength, we are on the solid mainland of purposeful sanity from which others can take their guidance from our luminescent dependability. In so beaming forth we exude an effulgent luminescence and incandescence that none can ignore or undervalue. By shining a light on things we sharpen and intensify them. Taking them out of the darkness enables us to show what can be done with them.

Thus, we serve humanity well by being a beacon of light that brightens up people's lives. To that extent, everyone is a potential illuminist though no one is born to be so. We can learn to be illuminists by aspiring to be enlightening people so that we make a habit of it throughout our lives. Being illuminists enables us to relate to others in enlightening them and making more of their lives. It heightens our interest in and appreciation of other people. Illuminists are shining examples to others and are ever-ready to vindicate themselves through illumination and service. They illuminate others by their belief in humanity's future and by their steadfastness in that belief. They also learn by appreciating its opposite, as the illuminist can be contrasted with the melanist as the following table shows:

Illuminist	*Melanist*
Light	Dark
Positivist	Negativist
Optimist	Pessimist

There is a fervent need for us to make more of the Illuminist in us than the Melanist. This need comes from the vitality of our inner being. That vitality needs to be directed outwards in an enlightening way to prevent it from turning inwards and towards hellish darkness. Hell is not other people but the darkness within us. Thus, the outward-looking Illuminist is opposed the inward-looking Melanist who looks on the dark side of things. There is a Melanist in all of us since there is inevitably light and dark within us all. We owe it to ourselves to put our dark side behind us and look towards the light. To that extent, we are constantly at war with this darkness that threatens to envelope us and hinder our forward progress.

We are all inclined at various times to be positive and negative, optimistic and pessimistic depending on our circumstances. However, our well-being depends on our light side predominating over our dark side. We must fight for the light as against the darkness that would engulf it. It is not old age that needs to 'rage against the dying of the light' but young people who are even more vulnerable to the self-annihilation to which self-abnegating darkness leads them. In this battle, positive thinking and an optimistic demeanour can help us on the way. Smiles instead of scowls will win the day.

The role of the Illuminist. As light-seeking Illuminists we strive for illumination by clarifying things but not necessarily proving them beyond all doubt. We are always seeking greater clarity. We see ourselves as purveyors of light to the entire world. To see the light is to have something revealed to us that was previously mirky and impenetrable. To pour light on a subject is what every scholarly person strives to do in seeking truth. We enlighten and thereby lighten the burden of life by dispelling the darkness of ignorance, malice, hatred, bigotry, self-centredness, and so on. We are all purveyors of the light in so far as our lives bring the light of experience and understanding into the world. Past purveyors of the light include not only Moses, Jesus Christ, the Buddha, and Mohammed but also all the scientists who have contribute positively to scientific knowledge. Enlightenment is what we seek throughout life, whereas dimness and darkness is what we avoid throughout life. The light is thus common to us and is as important to the religious person as to the scientist. We do not worship the light but revere only what it can do for us and what we can do with it. Such reverence is enough to ensure that we use it well and not as a malignant cover for dark deeds.

The illuminating standpoint is an attitude of mind that we must cultivate lest the darkness and dullness of negative thinking should engulf us. In response, we illuminate the importance of living. In the darkness of negativity "*rien, rien n'avait d'importance*" (nothing, nothing matters). The same sentiment is expressed in the Bohemian Rhapsody pop song – "Nothing really matters anymore" and the even more pathetic "I wish I had never been born at all". But everything matters when we pour enough light on life and living to see that the fact of living is itself marvellous and miraculous. The gift of life overarches any negativity when we concentrate on its opportunities instead of its discomforts. Moreover, anything is better than nothing, and ultimately there is nothing in nothing so that it is nothing which is not of any consequence. In resisting such pointless negativity, it is a matter of attitude and not of facts, opinions or beliefs. It is deliberately turning one's thoughts in a positive direction. Thus, it takes effort, study and persistence to keep this dark side at bay and concentrate on the light within us.

The dark side lurks around always to be combated. Religion makes much of walking in the light but in life we cannot avoid the darkness as readily as is implied, for example, in the following Biblical passage:

> "Walk as children of the light. For the fruit of the light is in all goodness and righteousness and truth. . . . And have no fellowship with the unfruitful works of darkness, but rather reprove them. For it is a shame even to speak of those things which are done of them in secret. But all things that are reproved are made manifest by the light: for whatsoever doth make manifest is light." *New Testament*, Paul's 'Letter to the Ephesians', 5: 8-13.

There are inevitably things within us that need never see the light of day. It is part of being human that there is a dark side to all of us, just as shining a light on it is even more human. The more light we pour on things, the less room there is for darkness. The sun shines all day when we fly around the earth following its course above the clouds. The higher our thoughts, the brighter the prospect. The right attitude determines the altitude, and *vice versa*. Thus, we can live all our lives illuminated perpetually by the brightness of our thoughts and deeds, provided that we work hard enough to make it so. We fly with the light and leave the darkness straddling behind us.

We live like flames that shine brightly as they feed on flammable material. We burn brightly during our lives by feeding on the flame of life for as long as it lasts. As the flame runs out of material to burn, so we run out of time and energy and our lives are snuffed out like a dying flame. We are however extremely complex flames that shine further than any other flames around us. The effects of the heat and light generated by us have reverberations far beyond our little lives. In fact, they have a cosmic resonance that contributes to posterity in what we leave behind us.

Above all, the Light of the Cosmos within us illuminates our way. As the Bible teaches us:

> "You are the light of the cosmos (τὸ φῶς τοῦ κόσμου). A city on top of a hill cannot be hidden. No one lights a lamp to put it under a bowl but to put it on a stand, so that it shines for everyone in the house. Let your light so shine for everyone that they may see the good you do."
> *New Testament*, Matthew, 5: 14-16.

It affects us all equally and makes no distinction between us. It is not really the sun which makes life possible on Earth but the light produced by the sun. The Cosmic Light is more important and worthy of respect than the sun which is only one insignificant source of light in the universe's vastness. The Cosmic Light is belongs to the entire universe whereas the light of the sun is only pinprick in comparison. This takes us into the role of the cosmic holist which is dealt with below in the exercise eight.

We can actively seek illumination both for ourselves and others. We illuminate the way for others by the good deeds we do for them, as well as by thinking of them affectionately. If we remain lurking in the darkness this intimates a failure to be oneself and to make something of oneself. Negative thinking, cynicism, enslavement by drink or drugs, resorting to criminality, are examples of dark living. There is no evil in the darkness itself; it merely lacks light. Evil lies in thoughts, intentions and motivations being deprived of light, love, honesty, truth. We put the evil into darkness which is otherwise devoid of anything. We therefore dispel evil by going into the darkness to illuminate it.

We achieve illumination in numerous ways, for example, through insights, revelations, as well as through scientific research. Philosophers, scientists, theologians, poets, novelists, and mystics, all contribute to our illumination. Everything human and inhuman is illuminating in its way, as we need never allow anything to darken our way if we can find illumination in it. For example, dark deeds can be illuminating in revealing our limitations and what we ought not to do. Beacons of brightness exist everywhere to lighten our way if we only make the effort to find them. All our positive thoughts are illuminating in so far as our minds are enlightened and brightened by them.

Accentuating the positive means promoting positive things at the expense of negative ones. Illumination accentuates the positive in that it flows with life and therefore through non-life and not against it. Everything is slithered to the side in its forward, just as light photons are deflected by the gravitation of large objects in space. The light follows the line of being and is distinguishable from non-being in that it is goal-directed. It is not just a matter of opposing or combating either non-being or the negative. It is also a matter of pursuing a positive course of action which is ultimately the way of life and not the way of non-life. In this way, the illuminating view can ensure that judgments are made as to actions that are positive and not negative.

B. The Benefits of Illuminating Life

Illuminating Love: The Holy Light of love brings us all together for the highest purposes of humanity. Love lightens all our lives and brightens everything it touches but only when it is caring, thoughtful love. Love applies to our relationships with everyone and everything that interests and involves us and takes us out of ourselves. But love brings darkness as much as light when it is a means of captivating and imprisoning people. Love without care and affection darkens and diminishes our souls and those of others captivated by this lustful love.

Illuminating Knowledge: The Holy Light of Knowledge replaces the dark light of religion which has brought much suffering, ignorance and ignominy to humanity. Knowledge is holy and delightful because it gives reasoned meaning and purpose to our lives. Knowledge begins with self-knowledge which enables us not only to live with ourselves but also to appreciate each other. Through study, we begin to put our knowledge in its proper perspective. We gain knowledge through our personal involvement in it. Our interest and enthusiasm in getting to know and understand things is the source of the light that we throw on knowledge.

Illuminating Truth: The Holy Light of Truth comes to us when we see ourselves as being significant in relation to the unity of things. Truth

2. Illumination: Enlightening Everything

highlights the path before us by drawing us on and showing us a better way of doing things, thinking about them, acting on them, anticipating them. We use truth first of all to find ourselves, then to find how things are, and finally how we want things to be. We keep to the path of truth in being open-minded and by freely inquiring into things. An open mind pursues truth by pouring light on things and moving forward to greater enlightenment, whereas a closed mind remains stuck in the false darkness of self-centredness. The path of truth is fringed on both sides by error and ignorance that lead us to darkness and depression. Truth is not just what is said to be the case; it is more importantly what can be done. It is relational rather than absolute. We can approach it and try to keep up with it but it inevitably recedes before us. Those who think that they have truth to hand are only grasping dreams, shadows and falsities.

Illuminating the Present: Carpe diem: seize the day. The present time is the right time to do what must be done, correct what must be corrected, and help who must be helped. *Nunc stans*: the standing now which refers to constant presence of reality lying before and around us. It is also the *Dasein* – the 'being there' that stands still as time moves on inexorably. The everlasting now is what we must make the best of with the full force of our being. The 'Now' is happening for each of us only in so far as we make something of it. While we do nothing right now, we are a living death. We are marking time instead of going along with it. We do not exist in the present so much as endure it. Our lives are prolonged for the duration of our existence but not forever.

Illuminating the Darkness:

> "The eye is the lamp of the body. If your eyes are good, your whole body will be full of light. But if your eyes are bad, your whole body will be full of darkness. If therefore the light within you is darkness, how great is that darkness!"   *New Testament*, Matthew, 6:22-23.

Seeing the light and avoiding the darkness takes effort and application. Darkness lingers on whenever things cease to move forwards. Everything that is stagnant and stuck in the doldrums is in gloom and darkness. All religions are in darkness in so far as they linger in the past and wield absolute power over people instead of empowering them. Mohammedism is the darkest religion of all as it gives all light to God, and leaves unbelievers in total darkness (see *The Koran*, Suras xxiv 35-36, iv 174, lxvi 8, lvii 28 etc.) It offers them only hell-bound annihilation. We avoid the darkness not by outward shows of belief (which invites hypocrisy) but by being true to ourselves and to others. Seeing ourselves as others see us is one form of inner illumination. We are never content with ourselves just as we are but seek ever to better and enlighten ourselves.

Illuminating the Future: In the future, everything that we do in the present will be illuminated and made plain to all. We can do no better in the present than to serve the needs of posterity and ensure its future. When we enlighten the future with our good deeds, posterity will benefit and hopefully reward us with their gratitude. The meaning of our existence could well be even more enhanced by what posterity makes of it than by what we ourselves have made of it. We illuminate the future by anticipating how posterity may judge our present actions. Posterity is therefore present with us when we look to the future to judge our deeds and thoughts.

3. Morality - Disciplining Ourselves

A. The Need for the Discipline of Morality

We need morality to give us rules for our conduct and boundaries within which to behave ourselves. Without such rules and boundaries, there are no limits to the inappropriate behaviour to which we may stoop. By learning to live within such moral confines we can become normal, trustworthy and hardworking people. We can freely adopt and practice the norms of society to become mature and responsible people who are ready to take our place in society. Wholesomeness is necessarily incomplete without a sound moral basis that makes us life-long moralists.

Unless we learn to discipline ourselves and behave in a manner becoming to ourselves, we never can be moralists. The moralist wants to behave properly both for their own satisfaction and out of respect for other people. Such behaviour is self-reflective and can make us wise people. We cannot be wise unless we are living a basically moral life-style. This is a life-style that is restrained and self-regarding and is adopted by one's own freewill and not imposed willy nilly on us by others or society.

Morality is important because it is the means by which we distinguish between (1) behaviour that develops us and takes us forward and (2) behaviour that degrades us and lessens us. Personal development takes us forward while personal degradation weighs us down and cripples us as vibrant human personalities. We must discover for ourselves the behaviour that advances us as opposed to the behaviour that impedes us.

Moral behaviour involves self-discipline and self-direction. Without these, we dissipate and waste our vital energy. Within the context of morality we examine ourselves and come to terms with our inclinations to behave badly or inappropriately. It involves the studied exercise of self discipline wherein we discipline and direct our impulses, instincts, forces, and drives, and wherein we criticise our behaviour, motivations, inclinations, feelings, impulses and everything else that governs our behaviour and our relationships with other people and society in general.

Being a moral person means taking account of other people's feelings and thinking about the consequences of our actions on other people as well as ourselves. We do this by evaluating our own behaviour more than that of others. Thus, morality in this context is about personal evaluation and not about moralising about other people's behaviour. It is about what I ought to do rather than what you ought to do. We are not moralising for other people as it is about learning personal evaluation for ourselves. It is a process of self-education in which we learn the moral truth about ourselves. This enables us to consolidate our values and integrity and to establish the extent of our self-discipline and the commitment that is required to further our intelligence and creativity. The quest for moral truth involves making moral judgments and distinguishing right from wrong, good from bad, just from unjust. Otherwise we are no longer being true to ourselves and we become immoral or amoral. Immorality is not adhering to one's moral norms, and amorality is not having any moral norms to live up to. In short, a moralist is one who learns to exercise self-restraint by habit and choice.

Another task is to purify our actions and motivations by simplifying them. In place of lives complicated by meaningless and enervating self-indulgence we reduce our behaviour to what is truly necessary for our purposes. We seek the purity of balanced thinking that looks ahead to better things. It therefore means simplifying our lives by cutting out extraneous behaviour, habits, thoughts and other unwholesomeness and superfluous activities. The aim is not to impose austerity for its own sake but to maintain a balanced enjoyment of life instead of being subject to the vapid extremes of misery on the one hand and mindless ecstasy on the other hand. Thus, morality contributes to wisdom through the quest for moral truth and balanced living. In this way we become moralists who have the self-command needed to direct our passions instead of being ruled by them.

There are therefore distinct benefits in being a moralist. It means being a mature and responsible person making the best use of our intelligent and creative powers to live truthful and balanced lives. Responsibility involves taking account of the effects of our behaviour on other people. As moralists we take responsibility for our own lives. We become control freaks in the best possible sense. We establish control over our lives for the benefit of others as well as ourselves. This does not mean imposing our moral values on others simply because they behave differently from what we expect or find tolerable. It is what we impose on ourselves in being moralists, and it is not doing what we know we could do as we prefer on moral grounds not to do it. It requires strength of will not to do just what we feel like doing. We also control feelings lest we do unnecessary harm to other people. The inner strength to do so does not come naturally; it comes with maturity and is bolstered by the responsibility that life demands of us.

The self-disciplined moralist doesn't just conform mindlessly to social norms of behaviour. Being a moralist means relying on ourselves for self-discipline. We learn for ourselves how to do, say and think the right things. We aim to become moral people who do not act impulsively and thoughtlessly and who do not do or say the first thing that comes to mind. This is best achieved by a morality of self-evaluation by which we monitor and criticise our own behaviour. This is only possible when our inner being has been developed to the extent that we behave well because we want to. Thus, our moral behaviour consists in exercising self-restraint and self-regulation for the best possible purposes that are worthy of ourselves and humanity. A prerequisite is that we achieve sufficient self-knowledge to know our strengths and weaknesses in moral matters.

The moral view explicates the good and the truth and what are outlined here are only snippets that remain to be developed into a systematic theory of interactive ethics. The aim is to offer tools for achieving self-knowledge in ethical matters. In particular, interacting between extremes is shown to be a way of keeping on the straight and narrow. However, it is not good enough just to be a good person. Being good may involve doing nothing at all. Once we start doing things we need ways of evaluating our behaviour. Ultimately, the truth of what we are consists in what we do for others, humanity and the universe. We learn to see that truth within ourselves in interacting with other people and society as a whole. Moral evaluation is a useful guide in assessing whether we are really being affectionate, showing respect towards others, acting honourable, and so on. But a prerequisite to acquiring such moral skills is the possession of 'moral sense' which is now outlined.

B. The Role of Moral Sense

Moral sense gives us self-awareness and self-criticism. In so far as morality is an internal more than an external matter, it concerns our 'moral sense'. This is a product of the inner being which is our introspective mental activity as is explicated with regard to the Vitalist's role above. Moral sense is basically our conscience or 'superego' (to use Freud's word). It consists in being aware of the inner voice telling us to desist from doing what it is feels to be undesirable or avoidable. It is inner being turning in on itself to make us aware of our behaviour and its merits and demerits. In practical terms, we stop to think and assess our behaviour. It makes us morally sensitive of our conduct and we feel shame or guilt if that conduct has not met with our inner approval. If we are mature and responsible adults, we don't need to be told what we know 'in our hearts' we should not do. We learn to 'desist and resist' as far as our inclinations are concerned. Nothing needs to be specified by any external authority that claims to know us better than we know ourselves. When we begin to think for ourselves we need to develop morality for ourselves by our inner development. Hence the importance of inner being in helping us to regulate our conduct.

Morality therefore begins with our moral sense which is partly inborn and partly acquired. It is the intuitive product of our inner being which itself is partly inborn and acquired. Because moral sense is basically intuitive, what is given by it is not enough in itself make us moral let alone rational. Our moral sense may rouse us to be angry, indignant, sympathetic, appreciative, or have other feelings, regardless of whether we have real reason or evidence to support such feelings. To that extent, we are slaves to our passions and can be provoked into hasty actions for no reason at all. However, we can learn to discipline ourselves by interacting critically with what is given by our moral sense to make us consistent in our behaviour, and give ourselves moral direction in the conduct of our lives. Thus, our moral sense is given us by intuition but is trained and disciplined by reason which consists in putting our feelings into words and relating them to our purposes as a whole. The holistic exercises are intended to helpful in ascertaining these purposes.

Having a moral sense means being directly cognisant of one's feelings. It involves intuition and direct sensitivity rather than reason, calculation or verbal expression. We are directly aware of our feelings without having arrived at them by any conscious process. Having experienced these feelings we then interact with them and make them the subject of our reasoning powers. We need to react in that way, otherwise we are enslaved by our emotions rather than master of them. Some of the feelings connected with moral sense are listed as follows:

Approval Feelings	Disapproval Feelings	Responsive Feelings	Susceptible Feelings	Refined Feelings
Gratitude	Contempt	Sympathy	Guilt	Purity
Appreciation	Anger	Compassion	Shame	Uprightness
Reverence	Disgust	Empathy	Embarrassment	Integrity

A Table of Moral Sensibilities

Approval feelings reflect our recognition of other people's forbearance, altruism or excellence. They prompt us to reward these traits in other people. Such feelings need to be cultivated and expressed to foster our social relationships. They help us to be less selfish and self-centred in showing how we value and appreciate the other people's behaviour towards us regardless of whether we consider their responses to be more or less appreciative than we deserve.

Disapproval feelings are expressive of the indignation that we feel at other people's behaviour, though they may also result from annoyance at our own behaviour. At worst, these feelings can prompt us to seek vengeance and find ways of punishing the infractors. At best, they help us inform others of the extent to which we disapprove of their behaviour, and to clarify to ourselves our disapproval of our own behaviour.

Responsive feelings result from seeing others in plights that we would wish to avoid ourselves. We respond to the inner anguish of other people because we can put ourselves in their position. These feelings take us out of ourselves and help us to put ourselves in other people's shoes.

Susceptible feelings follow from the disapproval that we feel about our actions which we would like to be otherwise than what they are. Being ashamed of our behaviour helps us to regulate and discipline it. Thus, for example, we may feel guilt and shame at our sexual behaviour and we can use these feelings to impose more discipline upon ourselves. But the discipline must come from within and not be imposed from without.

Refined feelings. These feelings most distinguish us from other animals that are incapable of such refinement. They are resonant of our attempts to behave to the highest standards and to be better people as a result. Thus, these feelings flow from our desire to regulate our behaviour in relation our highest and best aims and purposes. They are holistic feelings that transcend our animality and give us divine aspirations that are too easily projected outside us as divine beings or inside us as divine delusions of grandeur. These feelings therefore need to be restrained and disciplined as any others.

There can be no self-restraint or inner discipline without moral sense. For it enables us to be sensitive to the wrongness of bad behaviour in ourselves and others, and being susceptible to feelings of disgust, anger, shame and guilt about such behaviour. Some acts are simply repugnant to us because they do not feel right. Such feelings are the product of inner being and go to the heart of what we are as human personalities.

The lack of moral sense may have a genetic basis. Some people may be born deficient in moral sense, for instance, because of damage to their genes, and some may be lose it through bad upbringing or adverse circumstances. Others may decide for their own reasons that they don't want to be sociable or amenable persons. They will not allow themselves to be sensitive to the feelings of others, or to feel adversely about whatever nasty or unacceptable behaviour they may indulge in. Thus, sociopaths, psychopaths and other anti-social or totally misanthropic individuals are typically devoid of moral sense. But whether they actually commit anti-social or criminal acts is another matter. If they are clever or self-regarding enough, they may appear to be socially respectable and their propensities may never be made evident.

The presumption must be that everyone is capable of moral sense until their total lack becomes apparent and they are shown to be constitutionally irremediable, and perhaps need to be locked away for life. Nevertheless, self-control must be possible in an otherwise normal person.

Even though a person is genetically deficient in their moral sense, their ability to exercise self-control and consciously refrain from immoral or socially unacceptable conduct must be presumed. Overall, such defective individuals may need to be specially trained and disciplined to alter their ill-natured feelings. Quite simply, it is in their self-interest to behave themselves and this needs to be made clear to them. No one with any sense wants to be considered so abnormal that they are not expected to behave themselves and consequently must be deprived of the free and open life-style that the rest of us take for granted.

A loss of moral sense can result from self-indulgence and depravity. It means losing touch with one's inner monitor. Self-control and self-discipline are impaired. As a result, there is a lack of guilt, shame and remorse at one's conduct and over the results thereof. Kleptomaniacs and sex addicts are typically lacking in moral sense in so far as they have lost control over their behaviour. Such a deficiency means that they need to work harder than most people to make themselves socially viable human beings. Prisons and other social institutions need to be properly equipped to help people by training and disciplining them in a manner that is shown to be effective and appropriate. In these ways, lack of self-control can be countered by education and training. Thus, the ability to respect the interests of the community and of humanity as a whole is an essential extension of inner being by which it develops within itself to get beyond its innate self-centredness, as is now discussed.

C. Personal Interaction

Self-discipline involves balancing extremes of behaviour. To discipline ourselves, we must learn to interact with our impulses and inclinations and become aware of their power and potential. This interacting enables us to distinguish ourselves from these impulses and inclinations so that we do not give way to them immediately and thoughtlessly. We can learn more effectively to do this by becoming aware of the oscillation between our feelings of pride and humility. If we are overconfident then we give way to impulses all the more readily. If we lack confidence then we may go to the other extreme and become inhibited in respect of all our feelings. To avoid these extremes we need to be aware of when we are being too full of ourselves at one extreme and thinking too little of ourselves at the other extreme. We therefore learn to get the correct balance between pride and humility which will enables us to act and behave appropriately and rationally in all circumstances. The one extreme leads us to become overly active while the other extreme makes us overly passive, as is depicted in this interactive table:

PRIDE   ←   →   HUMILITY
⬇   ⬇

Self Expressing	Self Restraining
Empowering	Disciplining
Self Indulgent	Puritanical
Spendthrift	Parsimonious

⬇   ⬇

ACTIVE   ←   →   PASSIVE

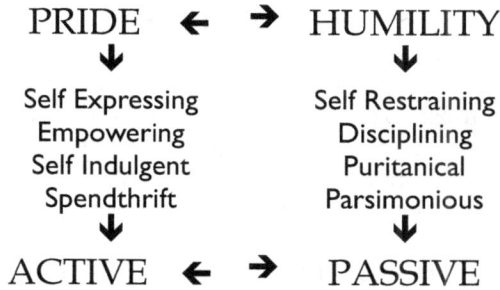

The Interactive Tension Between our Proud and Humble Propensities

Uncertainty as whether we are proud or humble, active or passive keeps us constantly re-assessing our situation. It is right that we should be unsure of whether we are superior to inferior to other people, and in what ways. To be utterly sure of our superiority or of our inferiority is to possess either a superiority complex or an inferiority complex. At such extremes, we look loftily down on people or meekly up to them. We are either too proud or too humble. The balanced personality is forever uncertain since this keeps us on the hop. If we are never too sure whether we are being proud or humble, we have to think carefully about it, that is to say, if we are concerned at all. We must balance our propensities towards superiority or inferiority and put restraints on our pride and humility. The balancing process is always ongoing and inconclusive.

We can consciously aim to be sociable and amenable persons as opposed to self-seeking, self-indulgent individuals. This is achieved by plotting the middle route between the extremes outlined above. We constantly battle to avoid entrapment at one extreme or the other. A mature and responsible person learns to find a healthy balance between self-expression and self-restraint. Thus, a maturation process is needed to cope with these extremes. Empowerment is potentially self-destructive if it is not restrained by self-discipline. If we want to, we can learn to avoid the extremes of being totally self-indulgent and totally puritanical, or totally spendthrift and totally parsimonious. We do so through experiencing those situations that lead us astray and how to avoid them in the future. Ideally, this maturation process should take place in adolescence and should be undertaken in full knowledge and understanding of these extremes and the harm that they can do to the individual.

A 'golden mean' between these extremes is not implied. There is no absolute or categorical mean between these extremes. There is only a fluid interaction between them. Most of our ethical dilemmas are rooted in our perennial uncertainty about whether to act or not act, to restrain ourselves or not restrain ourselves. Thus, we must learn to balance self-expression with self-restraint, self-indulgence with puritanism, and so on. This interactive balancing does not involve a 'golden mean' (to use Aristotle's phrase)[3] between these extremes as the middle route is constantly shifting and uncertain. We have to work hard to keep on the straight and narrow. There is no dogmatic answer always to be adhered to. The Aristotelian approach is overwhelmingly categorical and therefore too logically clear-cut to help us in those practical problems that require fine judgments and flexible thinking. The process of maturation cannot be reduced to a logical one of categorisation. It is an ongoing experience that is dynamic, interactive and cumulative over time. The more that we make of our experiences in life, the more we are equipped to deal adequately with whatever life throws at us.

The process of maturation is one of *personalisation* in which we become mature and responsible persons and know our place in the scheme of things by means of contextual self-awareness and ethical interactivity. We become sociable persons rather than isolated individuals. We are aware of ourselves as social beings and therefore capable of ethically assessing our behaviour. Thus, in personalising ourselves we adopt ethical values which initially are beyond ourselves in belonging to the language culture in which we are born more than to ourselves. These ethical values are established whenever we articulate our aims and goals in terms of the rational alternatives available in the society.

The quest for individuality often runs counter to that of personalisation in so far as it confines the individual to the context of self. Personalisation means embracing other contexts to be become a better person. We need individuality but only within the limits dictated by personalisation. This means becoming an individual who is also a respectable and well-adjusted person having a place and standing in society. This means balancing our pro-self and anti-self propensities as exemplified in the following diagram:

Pro-Self	*Anti-Self*
Pride	Humility
Love	Hatred
Pleasure	Pain
Beauty	Deformity
Pride	Humility

The Positive and Negative Aspects of Selfishness

A well-balanced person will therefore balance these two propensities which limit and channel our behaviour. Thus, balancing also means taking account of negative extremes as well as positive ones. There is no point in running away from or suppressing humility, hatred and the rest of the anti-self propensities as these are feelings that are a part of us as much as our more positive feelings. This view means taking account of negative and contrary feelings so that they can be rationalised in relation to our more positive feelings. Participating fully in society gives us our best chance of overcoming the negative and accentuating the positive. Thus, the holistic view of morality consists in directing our feelings towards sociable purposes without repressing them on the one hand or allowing them a free rein on the other hand. Holistic purposes are therefore important in directing us between these extremes. These purposes are ascertained in the following roles outlined below.

4. Humanism - Serving Humanity

A. How We Can Serve Humanity

We are all humanists by virtue of belonging to the human race. Not to be a humanist is to be barely human. The holistic role of the humanist is that of serving humanity, both as individuals and as a collective species. We value human beings and show that value by serving them. If we are wise we do not live for ourselves alone but enjoy serving and pleasing other people as well as ourselves. It is natural for us to commit ourselves to the service of other people. In a sense we are born to serve each other, and it is only human to make ourselves useful to each other. We normally do this quite naturally when we are getting something worthwhile in return for our servitude, for example, a good living wage. In serving other people we put them at the centre of our world. We start with individuals and work our way up to humanity as a whole. The individual is more important than humanity as every single human being is an indispensible part of humanity.

We cannot cut ourselves away entirely from other people without making ourselves less than human. We are joined to them in our common humanity. It is also natural for us to have fellow feelings for every human being on the planet and not allow our ideas, beliefs or opinions to diminish these feelings or lessen our view of them. The plight of each person on Earth is our common concern.

Service is not slavery as long as we are acting from own freewill and are being treated with the dignity and respect due to every human being. In that respect, being of service to others is fulfilling and liberating. When service stops being fulfilling and liberating then it is indistinguishable from slavery. But it all depends on how we see the role ourselves. We may willingly make slaves of ourselves and not think we are slaves. One of the unfortunate consequences of socialist/communist thinking was that servants were seen as making slaves of themselves. According to that view, we should all be equal as working human beings. It led to the unfortunate collapse of the serving class as prominent feature in our society. People were metaphorically turned out into the streets to fend for themselves, thus creating a society of loners. The leisure class is no longer composed only of rich people but also of poor people who live permanently on benefits. In contrast, a society in which people willingly become servants is more cohesive as people come together to live with and for each other. For example, the 17th century musketeers in Alexandre Dumas's novel *The Three Musketeers* are portrayed as each having their 'valets' who acted as servants, even when the musketeers themselves were as poverty-stricken as their servants.

The fact is that we are not all equal human beings and we thrive on our differences. Attempts to iron out our economic and social differences are bound to cause more grief than relief. We are all equal in being different from each other, and the fairest society maximises our opportunities to make the most of our differences without depriving anyone of their opportunities. A society based on our serving one another in one capacity or another arguably gives us all the best chance of attaining the ideal of equal opportunities for all. Too much emphasis on equality has the paradoxical effect of exacerbating competition between people as they strive to differentiate themselves in a society of undifferentiated equals. We need to work together, not against each other.

Co-operation is more important than competition. We have evolved to be a co-operative as well as a competitive species. We progress by balancing these two tendencies. But the unity and survival of society depends more on co-operation than on competition. Serving one another is the best way for us to co-operate towards the common ends of humanity. Our unity depends on a culture of service more than on a culture of competition. The most progressive periods in our history have been those in which service has been to the fore, even though other aspects of everyday life such as war, famine and plague might not have been so propitious. Therefore, co-operation is more important to our survival than competition. The latter only makes sense when we are vying with each other to better our service to others. The most successful organisations under capitalism are those that are more efficient in their service provision than in their profit-making. Internet companies such as Amazon and Google became successful because of the efficiency of their service and only later did they become exorbitantly profitable. The most popular organisations in the UK are the BBC and the National Health Service, neither of which make profits. Also, Wikipedia is obviously an entirely voluntary organisation whose service is universally used and appreciated.

We vindicate ourselves through serving the needs of other people, humanity and life forms in general. Our common humanity consists in making ourselves available for such services and this makes us feel that we belong and are a part of the whole. Also, our daily lives would be impossible without the service of others when we buy goods and services, seek to be entertained and so on. It is only right and just that we should serve others in our turn. Our very survival as a species depends our willingness to serve each other. Our civilisation would cease to exist if we all lived for ourselves alone like male orang-utans. When we know that other people are devoted to serving us honestly and to the best of their abilities, we can trust and rely on them unconditionally. Thus, service is a necessary prerequisite to trust and reliability in our social relationships.

Our security depends on other people being willing to be of service to us. For example, the idea of service to the community offers a way of tackling the problems of internet privacy, snooping, and exploitation. We would be more confident that internet organisations are acting in our best interests if their use of internet information is shown to be strictly in our service. Our interests must be paramount in the access and use of internet information about the people's personal lives and activities. These organisations should be obliged to keep us informed and to demonstrate periodically their commitment to this prime principle of service.

Counselling of all kinds helps people. We can serve our fellow human beings particularly well by counselling them. This may mean no more than giving them useful advice or giving them help to understand their problems better. It can therefore be performed either professionally or personally. In the past, it was left entirely to religious people to offer counselling to people. But this is increasingly unacceptable, especially when so many priests and clergy are shown to use their profession for their own personal, prurient purposes.

The tendency of religion is to counsel its servants to keep them enslaved to its orthodox beliefs. Its fault lies in making people the means to the end of religion instead of treating them as ends in themselves. Religion gives comfort by offering absolute certainties. In doing so, it does not help people inside themselves. A listening counsellor is liable to be more helpful with people's problems than the canting preacher.

Counselling is best performed by professionals who are trained and experienced in helping people. But as caring people, we can make ourselves useful in the counselling that we offer others in our daily lives, when they come to us in times of need. Counselling therefore serves humanity when it really and genuinely helps people. It may not do so if it is imposed on them as a matter of form. Not everyone wants or needs counselling and they should have a choice in the matter. Its role is diminished if it becomes compulsory or enforceable in any way. Then it no longer serves real needs but becomes a bureaucratic imposition that interferes with freedom of choice.

B. Serving Society

We serve society and it serves us in its turn. Throughout our lives we serve society in one way or another simply by being rational people doing reasonable things. This means behaving in a friendly and sociable way on most occasions, despite provocations or adverse distractions. By being sociable people we make society more tolerable for other people. Society is after all no more than all of us interacting together to get through our daily lives as comfortably and happily as we can. But it is also useful to think of our relationship to society in formal terms. We serve society and society serves us, so that, whether we like it or not, there is a formal relationship going on which only lacks a name. Also, serving others inevitably means serving society as every human relationship is a part of society as a whole.

In so far as we submit to the two-way service of society we enter into an implicit *civic covenant.* This is not to be confused with what was called a 'social contract' which was a legalistic concept to be imposed on the individual by the authorities. The civic covenant is here seen as a matter of individual choice. We enter this covenant on becoming socially responsible persons who choose to take their place in society as free citizens. In entering this covenant, we pay for our freedoms by taking on various obligations and responsibilities. In return, society gives us the facilities and organisations we need in living our lives freely and responsibly. In that way, the civic covenant involves two-way obligations – a give-and-take involving both society and the individual.

In giving of our best, we need to know where we stand and what is expected of us. To maintain the social structure, some basic obligations and responsibilities should be laid down. For instance, the right to freedom of self-expression may accompany an obligation to marry, have children and be responsible for raising a family. Such a promotion of normal family life secures a base for the healthy flourishing of the personality.

Moreover, the civil covenant has moral rather than legal force. We enter into the civic covenant of our own freewill. It is not to be enforced by society in any legal or authoritarian manner. It is only binding on the individual's conscience as it has moral rather than legal force. The civil covenant can be taught in schools so that it becomes the product of education and social expectation. It can help to sharpen up young people's moral sense and sensitivity in particular. Basically, it means behaving ourselves, being answerable to other people and in that way rationalise and socialise our behaviour. You are expected to behave in a sociable way and the civic covenant merely reflects that expectation. The civil covenant is only important from a legal point of view in that it obviates the need for endless prohibitive legal enactments that infringe our freedoms and turn society into a legalistic police state ruled by police, lawyers and judges. It can therefore contribute to our liberation from the restrictive legalism that is currently intruding into every part of our private lives. It does so by appealing to our moral sense and becoming part of our habits of thought instead of being imposed on us legally.

The civil covenant is therefore quite distinct from the age-old notion of a 'social contract'. From Hobbes onwards, this contract was a legal one in which individuals submitted to the authority of government for protection, justice and the rule of law. The civil covenant differs in being made by each individual with themselves and for themselves alone. Thus, the 'original contract' is not with groups combining for self-protection and justice (*vide* Hobbes, Locke, Hume, Rousseau, Kant, Rawls, Nozick, *et al*), but with our individual selves opting into society with all its obligations and responsibilities for our own personal purposes to reap the opportunities and benefits for oneself alone. In being part of the legal system, the social contract is imposed on people instead of being understood as being part of the way we live and take our part in society.

Anyone engaging in anti-social behaviour is not adhering to any social covenant but to their own selfish concerns that take no account of other people's interests. Thus, the source of anti-social behaviour can be seen in the individual's personal failings. It is not solely a matter of law-breaking but mainly a failure to see that it is in their own interests to serve society and thereby serve themselves. Terrorists, sociopaths and hardened criminals break the covenant by alienating themselves and making a personal war on society. They have lost all respect for society because they no longer see a place for themselves in it. If they are taught to see the benefits of society in the light of the social covenant, this may help to obviate their alienation. It clarifies the fact that anti-social behaviour is not in their overall interests as unique individuals having a unique role to play in society.

The civil covenant reflects that fact that moral progress comes from within and cannot be enforced by society. We also make moral progress in our expectations of each other's behaviour. For instance, it is no longer acceptable to behaviour for men to ill-treat or abuse women or children, or to treat them as sex objects. Also, we are no longer allowed to give way with impunity to our feelings and impulses like animals. These expectations are learnt by people as part of their education and social upbringing. Their minds become tuned to the expectations of society and there is no need for these expectations to be enforced by fear of authority or legalistic sanctions. Moral progress is possible but only to the extent that moral self-discipline is taught and appreciated by everyone as individuals.

C. Serving Posterity

Thinking from the perspective of posterity. The ultimate service is that which benefits posterity. To do that, we need to see things from the perspective of posterity. When we think about the future consequences of what we are doing, this is best done from that viewpoint. Posterity is either future generations or intelligent beings in the future who are capable of understanding us. The word 'posterity' refers to 'future or succeeding generations' and 'all of one's descendants'. It comes from the Latin *posteritas* meaning 'future generations', and from *posterus* or 'coming after'. By thinking about future generations we put ourselves in their shoes and see ourselves from their point of view. We must imagine that our lives become accessible to them so that they can judge us and our lives whether we like it or not. Thus, the idea of serving posterity gives us a powerful tool by which we can evaluate the importance or non-importance of what we are doing now.

The word 'posterity' is used here not only to comprise the generations and life-forms that succeed us in the future, it also refers to what we make of the future by planning to make it better than the past. For we increase our value as individuals by serving posterity. The very meaning of our existence is enhanced as much by what we imagine that posterity will make of our existence as by what we actually make of our lives. This enhancement results from our having entered the context of posterity as well as by our anticipating how posterity may judge our present actions. In other words, we are elevated into a higher perspective of our lives by contemplating posterity. We can then think of our most mundane activities as serving posterity even when we have decided to do nothing when doing something might have adverse consequences. Serving posterity therefore means that everything we do has consequences for posterity, whether for good or ill. Whether we like it or not, we are either serving the needs of posterity or not serving its needs in whatever we do. Our judgments should always have posterity in mind; the possibility of posterity cannot be overlooked, as it is the ultimate vindication of all our efforts.

In this context the word posterity refers to future consequences and what we make of the future in the present. For our present actions have meaning for posterity whether we are aware of it or not. Making ourselves aware of posterity means bringing future generations to mind who will have to live with the consequences of what we do in the present. Future generations are important to us because everything we do now has some consequence to posterity. All our rational and purposeful activities gravitate towards the context of posterity within which the value of those activities is ultimately assessed, whether we like it or not. Everything that we do now, at this very moment, has some future meaning which cannot be ascertained in the present. We must pass on to posterity the task of judging what we do in the present. All we can do now is try to put ourselves in their shoes and make the best judgments we can.

The fact is that all our everyday actions have consequences for posterity. Most of us most of the time give little thought to posterity. Yet every meaningful thing that we do means something for posterity. When we do something, such as buy a new car, we do it in the immediate present but the effect of our action is in the future. The money spent on the car goes into the economy, helps to pay people's wages, supports the car industry, and so on. If the car is more fuel efficient and less polluting, it reduces our travelling expenditure and is less harmful to the climate. Thus, whatever we do, it has consequences for the future whether or not we intend that there should be consequences. Future generations will either benefit or not benefit from what we do in the present. What we do now therefore has meaning for posterity, assuming that future generations will survive in the future.

If an action is meaningful to us, it will also mean something, either the same or different, in the future. When a house is renovated, those who take over the house in the future will live with the consequences of that renovation. Any long-term benefits from what we do will benefit from posterity and this gives added meaning and value to these actions. Likewise, posterity will suffer because of our shortcomings which may have adverse effects beyond our imagination. It is thus very important to judge our actions from the perspective of posterity, which can suffer from our oversights. People in the future will think badly of us in so far as we fail to do our best for them.

Posterity is not just an imaginary notion. When we think of the future we inevitably use our imagination. But the notion of a posterity awaiting us in the future is more than just imaginary. The notion is backed up, firstly, by the evidence of evolution on this planet and, secondly, by the very real possibility of advanced species living elsewhere in the universe. If the human race autodestructs or is annihilated, other living species such as insects or rodents may evolve into intelligent beings who can peer back into the past. Also, intelligent beings are probably evolving elsewhere in the universe and they may visit the Earth in the far future, (as depicted, for example, in Spielberg's 2001 feature film, *A.I. Artificial Intelligence*). Thus, what I mean here by 'posterity' includes all these possibilities, and is not just confined to our descendants in the future. Whether posterity is composed of humans, other species, aliens, androids, or computer-generated holograms, posterity will still be interested in what we do here and now. Whether we develop or fail to develop further because of our self-destruction, they will want to know the reasons why, just as we are interested in past civilisations and why they ceased to exist. At the very least, they will want to avoid the mistakes we have made in the present.

Posterity in the form of intelligent beings elsewhere in the universe is highly probable because intelligence is a natural consequence of the complexification of the universe's contents. Material bodies organise themselves into ever more complex entities by interaction and intermixture. Eventually, entities become complex enough to have lives of their own. And by interacting with their environment, such life-forms become still more complex over time. They organise themselves into communities whose cultures complexify eventually into civilisations such as our own. Cultures of sufficient complexity will produce intelligent participants, and we can expect intelligence to emerge wherever life produces complex, social beings. As there are billions of galaxies in the universe with billions of stars in each of them, the chances are that there are millions of civilisations throughout the universe. Thus, the existence of posterity in some form seems to be just as assured as the existence of any form of life in the universe.

We must work to ensure a future posterity. However, all we can do at present to ensure that there is a posterity by our working to ensure the future of humanity. We cannot afford to sit back and wait for an alien intelligent species to arrive and take our place in the cosmos. Just as parents invest their time and energy in ensuring a future for their children, so we as a species must invest all our resources in our future prospects because our descendants depend on it. Ultimately we serve ourselves best by serving the purposes of posterity. Only such service can save us in spite of ourselves as long as we work hard to serve posterity by doing things that benefit the future and make for a better future.

Broadly speaking, posterity is the culmination of all human ends. When we look to the far future, we enter the context of posterity. We can see nothing remaining of humanity unless we are succeeded by a viable posterity in the form of generations of people who will take humanity forward to a better future. Within that context we can make judgments about the consequences of our present actions. We must imagine what posterity will make of what we are doing in the present. The problems of society can only be solved in the future, and when we imagine them as they will appear to future generations, we are considering in the context of posterity. However, our thoughts of the future may be mistaken unless they are also considered within such contexts as universe, life and humanity. Within these contexts we can reach the most realistic view of matters by making use of our hard-earned past experiences when things have turned out contrary to our expectations. While the other contexts can also be depicted as containing all the others, depending on the circumstances in which they are used, posterity is ultimately the most important of all and the most of in need of over-containment rather than under-containment.

This view of posterity enables us to re-interpret the 'hereafter' as being the life of future generations that continues after our death. It gives us the possibility of an 'afterlife' of sorts. But this is not experienced by us in any shape or form since we no longer exist physically. We may have a kind of afterlife if people living in the future are able to reconstruct our lives and relive them for their own interest in the same way that we watch films and videos today about past events. We live on potentially only in so far as our lives are accessible to posterity. But this is only our lives as we have lived them in their past. They may relive our lives only in so far as their knowledge and technology allows them to do. They are unlikely to become us in merely re-running our lives as they will be unable to interfere with the things that we have already done in their past.

The Great Day of Judgment awaits us all in posterity wherein we will all be judged according to what we have or have not done in our lives. We will not be personally called before the tribunal of posterity to account for our failings, but our lives will be. In leaving these lives behind us to be judged by in the future, we can never be sure how they will be judged. But we can be sure that traces will be left behind of our having lived, and of how we lived, and that these traces may be sufficient to enable our lives to be evaluated one way or another. Therefore, posterity will judge us whether we like it or not. We are all 'doomed' in that respect.

5. Optimism - Believing in the Future of Humanity

A. Believing in Humanity

There is a hole in the holistic view if it does not include belief in humanity and its future. Practically everything that we do has some future consequences and that implies at least some belief in our future. The optimistic view goes further and assumes that humanity has a good chance of surviving into the far future. The chances of our being obliterated by comets, solar flares or other cosmic catastrophes are fairly slim. But the optimist expects humanity not to stupidly destroy itself through its own malevolent self-destructiveness. There is also the optimistic belief in the inevitable propagation of life throughout the universe and in our potential role in contributing to that propagation. Belief in humanity and its future is a prerequisite to that propagation since we are at present the only hope of it taking place at all. Such beliefs are fundamental but they are not absolute as they are contingent upon our actually doing things to ensure our future. They are also contingent on humanity being worthy of any future at all. Its deserving to have any future has always been in doubt. We always need to work hard to justify our existence on this planet.

These are not just matters of opinion. They are empirical matters which may be shown to be case by careful and impartial consideration of the facts. It is a fact that humanity has developed the ability to look into the future and question whether it can survive into the far future. When we look at the state of humanity at any point in time its future has always been in doubt. Plagues and other natural catastrophes have decimated our species, yet it has survived even though the odds may have been stacked against it. Whether we will continue to survive and thrive is always a matter of probability. But we can always find reasons for optimism if we want to find them. Whether we deign to face the fact that we will probably survive into the future is also a matter of choice.

There is no point in being wise unless it is for some purpose beyond ourselves. In the absence of any credible supernatural being, that purpose must involve a worthwhile contribution to humanity and its future. If we do anything meaningful in our lives, it is in the implicit expectation that it will have meaning in the future and that humanity will survive in the future. There is no need for anyone to explicitly believe in humanity's future. That belief is implicit in everything we do whether we are conscious of it or not. If what we do makes sense to others then we are taking part in human affairs by doing rational and sensible things. The fact of being a human being, who takes part in the activities of the human race, is also an implicit acknowledgement of this belief. No one needs to be put to the test about this as it is plain in the actions of even the most sceptical or misanthropic of people. If they behave rationally and do human things in their everyday lives, they show themselves to be as human as the rest of us.

Thus, believing in humanity is necessary whether it is implicit or explicit. The whole of humanity depends on everyone contributing in their own small way to that whole. We cannot make such contributions unless we think at least occasionally in global terms, as we do, for example, in the various anti-poverty campaigns and in our concerns for the victims of earthquakes, tsunamis, floods and famines. These arguments therefore show the importance of our getting together to ensure our own future.

The dualist nature of humanity. The notion of humanity is not just inclusive of every human being. It consists in what the individual human being contributes to it and what it can do for the individual in return. The interaction between these is what makes the human race work. Humanity is only an idea or notion and is not more important than the individual person. Our contribution to humanity is what we do in making the most of what we are as individual human beings. What humanity can do for us is to give us the opportunity to do our best as human beings. This includes our rights and responsibilities as mentioned in respect of the Civic Covenant mentioned above. Thus, humanity is not an end in itself but a means of benefiting us all as individuals. It ceases to benefit us in so far as it lets anyone down unnecessarily.

Why should we worry about the future of humanity, let alone believe in it? Most people never think about it from one day to the next. We are too concerned about our own present worries. The idea that humanity as a whole has a future, as opposed to the future of our respective races, nations, religions, organisations or other divisions, does not loom large among our concerns. Yet our everyday lives depend on the human race moving forward to better things. If we don't progress we will regress to a worse kind of society. The forward movement unites us as a species and we make progress because the sense of direction gives us a common purpose. Without that, we will fall apart and start fighting each other as has happened so often in the past, and is still happening in many parts of the world even today. Working together to secure humanity's future gives us a common purpose, as does spreading life beyond Earth.

The worry is that, as a species, we can regress very easily to a more primitive state. If the idea of humanity fails to unify us, our society will sooner or later disintegrate into antagonistic units – nations competing to destroy other nations – religions fighting against other religions – races exterminating other races. There is no limit to the regression of humanity to more primitive conditions if we lose contact with each other and become insular groups that gradually forget their past traditions and ways of doing things. The Tasmanian aborigines and the Tierra Fuegans, whom Darwin mentions in his book *The Voyage of the 'Beagle'*, are examples of how isolated groups can lose their skills and forget how to fish and make fire. Archaeological evidence clearly shows that their ancestors had these skills in their dim and distant past. Anthropological research, such as in the book *The Mountain People*, shows the mechanisms of increasing distrust and over-self-sufficiency leads to the breakdown of social structures and a regression of a more primitive form of society in which the rules of morality are forgotten. In western Europe, the loss of literature and culture during the Dark Ages was brought about by excessive religious fanaticism which emptied the cities and filled the countryside with monasteries and nunneries, as Gibbon pointed out. People ceased to care about humanity or its future and they lived only to serve a pitiless non-existent entity that does nothing for us. Thus, religion regresses and demeans us when it is pursued fanatically and mindlessly.

There is no substitute for self-belief. Belief in our future is essential to our survival as a species. Nothing outside ourselves in any way guarantees our future. However, it is arguable that our inner resources are strong enough to ensure our future, barring unforeseeable natural catastrophes coming from comets, solar flares and the like. This book begins the task of demonstrating the strength of these resources. Thus, there is no need for faith in God, aliens, angels or whatever, as our faith in ourselves and our future is all that we require. We can go beyond ourselves without invoking supernatural presences. Contributing to posterity gives us goals that serve the future instead of the dead past as in the case of religion. It is also argued in this book that we contribute to the Cosmos in our making sense of ourselves and our environment.

We have no choice but to take responsibility for ourselves since there is no concrete evidence of anything else in the universe that has the slightest regard for us. This is not a depressing fact but a challenge to us to justify our existence against all the odds. We can easily think ourselves into extinction, never mind all the external and internal threats to our future. Indeed, it is now fashionable to doubt that humanity has any future at all. We could exterminate ourselves in by self-inflicted means such as a nuclear war that is precipitated by economic collapse or by conflicts over ever-diminishing resources or such as diseases concocted by deluded scientists. There are also lots of external threats that will do the business. We could be wiped out entirely by pandemics, comets, solar radiation or whatever our fertile imaginations can conjure up.

It is often assumed that because all civilisations in the past have collapsed sooner or later, ours is bound to follow suit. However, past civilisations were localised whereas ours now spans the globe. It is arguable that as the world civilisation develops and strengthens through globalisation, it is equipped better than ever to deal with local collapses and catastrophes. If Europe, America and Asia were to collapse economically, the whole of Africa and Australasia may still survive the cataclysm and slowly revive the world economy.

Certainly, if we wait long enough any number of catastrophes could befall us. However, our survival as a species depends on self-belief. Once we stop believing in ourselves and our future, we deserve to become extinct. Survival means fighting for ourselves and this means finding reasons for our existence on this planet. We need to continually seek such reasons to reassure ourselves about our mission. Thus, our survival depends on finding reasons to survive and on staving off negative thinking to the contrary.

One of the biggest threats to our future at this time is a looming financial collapse due to unsustainable levels of debt throughout the world. An increased unity of nations and a reduction of national sovereignty seem necessary to organise the financial structure and eliminate debts. There is bound to be a rational solution if we work hard enough to find it. But an irrational response might result if we allow nations and organisations to compete and impose their own solutions on each other. This could lead to conflict, war and possible nuclear annihilation. Another rational alternative is for us to populate the moon and other planets, and use their resources to pay off our debts. These rational alternatives will be overlooked unless we response to our problems as a co-operative, unified and purposeful species. In short, we need to believe in our future as a unified species. This book aims to drive home the imperative need to achieve such a unity of purpose and direction for all humanity.

There is nothing religious about this belief. Believing in humanity does not mean worshipping it or putting it on a pedestal. It is a matter of taking a realistic view of what we are and what we can do together. We serve humanity in acting together for the benefit of everyone. As individuals, we serve humanity by being ourselves and by behaving ourselves. This means doing the best we can and being on our best behaviour at all times since posterity is always on the watch for us.

Our belief in ourselves is not sacrosanct but must be continually justified by our meaningful thoughts and actions. Our self-belief is subordinate to our understanding of ourselves and not *vice versa* as in the case of religious belief, which makes us believe that we are the image of God. This flatters us unduly. The more we understand about the human condition the more we have concrete and realistic grounds for believing in what we are or are not as individuals and as a species. We need not believe in ourselves absolutely but only self-critically. Nothing else exists apart from ourselves that is capable of being understood without getting lost in vain fantasies and imaginings that corrupt our intellect and hence our morals. God belief is absolute and uncritical; it permits us to think anything we like since whatever occurs to us intuitively is assumed to come from God rather than from our unconscious selfish desires. The humanist approach stresses the importance of starting from ourselves outward rather than starting from something outside ourselves which can only be imagined to exist.

Holism aims to bring us together. Holism is a philosophy to be understood rather than a religion to be adhered to. It is basic enough to be common to all humanity regardless of their religious beliefs or the lack of them. It constitutes a means of unifying humanity to ensure its future. To that end, it is necessary to transcend all viewpoints that divide us from each other. These viewpoints include the sectarian, national, racial, and religious divisions that are liable to set us against each other when they are treated as being more important than the interests of humanity as a whole.

B. How Humanity is Important

We only choose to believe we are unimportant. Many people scoff at the thought that humanity has any importance whatsoever. They may argue that way as much as they like but arguing does not make it so. The evidence can be interpreted as much from one viewpoint as from the opposite one. Such detractors are over-impressed by our cosmic insignificance in the face of an unimaginably huge universe. Like Hitler, they think of the human being as nothing but "eine lächerliche Weltraumbakterie"- 'a ridiculous cosmic bacterium'. He had contempt for the human race, life, and for everything except the fulfilment of his own grandiose ideas, as is evidenced by his role in history. As regards the human condition, we can be in two minds on the matter and, like Hamlet, regard ourselves as 'the beauty of the world, the paragon of animals' and at the same time nought but a 'quintessense of dust'. The correct attitude surely is to take account of both views – both the pessimistic and optimistic views of our future. Total pessimism can't be right and complete optimism can't be either. We necessarily oscillate between the two extremes while making the best of the present. It is not certain whether the human race has a future or not but we can carry on regardless in the expectation of better things to come. Believing in future possibilities is all important.

We are only as important as we think we are. Our self-belief depends on our interpretation of the facts. If a person takes the pessimistic view too seriously then all the facts are inevitably interpreted from that point of view. The balanced view avoids such lop-sided thinking. One's life is only as trivial as one thinks it to be. But thinking does not make it so. It is only an opinion based on the facts. The same facts can be interpreted equally well in the other direction and used to support the opinion that one's life is not trivial. A balanced look at the facts is attempted in this book.

Some ways in which we are important. Humanity's primary mission is to make more of the universe than hitherto. It is primary in the sense that it is the default position from which we must begin in defining our role on this planet. If we don't do anything else as a species we will have justified our existence. We are important in that respect because as far as we know at this time we alone are capable of doing this. In particular, we are also important at least in the following respects:

➢ We are important also because we are now responsible for the future of this planet and all the life-forms on it. No other species on Earth is competent to take on that role though we are ourselves diffident about taking on that role. We need to be much more organised in our handling of the planet and that entails much greater political integration and a greater purposefulness in what we do.

➢ We are important because we are increasingly unified as a species so that we can now communicate instantaneously with each other across the globe in a clear and unambiguous way that no other species can rival. This unity is spoilt by the national, religious, economic and language divisions which limit the extent to which we can communicate information.

➢ We are important as we are responsible for the next stage of evolution, namely, the machine age in which computers become increasingly intelligent and possibly self-regarding. We must be prepared to control of this situation and make sure that the value and importance of biological life is not overwritten by this development.

➢ We are important because we are the medial species between the very small and very large aspects of the universe. We are thus in a sense still at the centre of the universe even though it does not revolve around us. Our importance therefore lies in knowing that we are thus placed and in the increasing knowledge that we are acquiring about the very large and small aspects of the universe. (See the role of the scientist below for more on this centrality – especially page 66 onwards.)

➢ We are important because we bring value, meaning and purpose and into being that does not exist otherwise. As far as we know nothing else in the universe can find any value, meaning, or purpose in it to the extent that we are doing in making sense of the universe and of everything in it.

> We are important because we can put ourselves into context and thereby see our faults as well as our good points. We can use contexts to humble ourselves as well as elevate ourselves, but it is only through practised contextualisation that we can arrive at a realistic view of what we are and what we can do.

> We are important because our quest for knowledge and understanding contributes to the cosmos which consists in the continuous ordering of the universe and the consolidation of its contents, as is mentioned below concerning the cosmos and role of the holist.

> We are important in that we are responsible for ensuring that there is a posterity which will be capable of looking back and seeing what we have or have not done for their benefit.

C. What That Belief Entails

Humanity is a self-referential term. The notion of humanity does not exist as a thing but only as a self-referential term by which we refer back to ourselves as a species. There is no need at all for us to deify this notion since it is only a way thinking of ourselves. By its use, we can think of ourselves both critically and reverentially. We can see our strengths and weaknesses and do something about them. Only by such self-examination can we understand our place in the universe and hence where we are going and how we can get there.

We should therefore refer to humanity but not defer to it. Humanity is not an object of worship but a notion to which we can refer in considering our role in the universe and how we can unify ourselves to fulfil that role in the future. It is a point of reference and not an object of reverence. As a reference point it unifies us as a species. There is nothing to revere about humanity; we are too well aware of our defects and limitations as a species. It is no more than a context that we enter into and it is no more important than any other context in life. Its importance varies according to our situation and depends entirely on our individual judgment.

Love of humanity humanises us. Our love of people, animals, activities and objects takes precedence over love of humanity as an abstract notion. Love of humanity cannot mean murdering, injuring, threatening people or making their lives miserable. The latter are indicative of hatred of humanity. We are humanised by loving humanity in general when we identify with people in general by means of that notion. However, we can be dehumanised by loving humanity only as an abstract ideal that overlooks people altogether. Sacrificing people to further an idea or vision of humanity is characteristic of callous ideologies. Clearly, people are more important than ideas so that the idea of sacrificing the life of any person for an idea is anathema to the humanist view. However, we are humanised by the idea of humanity when it is applied as a way of making more of people and of benefiting them as individuals.

Belief in humanity and its future is a rational and practical belief compared with religious beliefs because it is focused on benefiting individuals. The more we are organised globally to care and cater for each other, the better life is for everyone. Business, trade and commerce cannot thrive without an implicit belief in humanity in respect of people's dependability, honesty and integrity. Without faith in people and their trustworthiness, our respective economies throughout the world must flounder. In contrast, religious beliefs can hinder enterprise by reducing people's self-confidence and their will to better themselves. Indeed, they undermine business activity and beggar people unless they are tempered with humanity and common sense. Around the world, even today, wherever religion has taken over and repressed secular activity, it has also abused human rights, reduced economic activity and undermined prosperity.

Believing in humanity also means acknowledging our moral superiority over other animals. This is the morality underlying our belief in humanity. Human beings are distinct from other animals in not having a fixed nature that compels us to act without thinking of the consequences. Other animals may behave largely instinctively and without self-restraint, whereas we can put thought and restraint into our behaviour. Therefore, it is in our nature *not* to do what comes natural to us. This is because our behaviour is culturally determined to a large extent, and we acquire self-respect and self-discipline because it is in our interests to do so. We don't need any religion to enforce morality upon us. Our culture determines the range of behaviours available to us. We are free to choose within that range what we want to do or nor to do with ourselves. As a result, animal behaviour and the behaviour of primitive human beings tell us very little about what it is to be human. Such behaviour is more likely to be of the sort that we want to avoid. It is not at all exemplary.

Moreover, believing in humanity means countenancing all aspects of human behaviour. The ancient Roman playwright Terence famously wrote "I am a human being: I consider nothing human alien to me." This is usually interpreted from a liberal point of view to express approval of immoral behaviour that comes naturally to us. However, it can equally be applied to behaviour that is unbecoming to us as human beings. In other words, it also expresses approval of moral behaviour as being 'human'. What it really means is that we should be prepared to consider the whole gamut of human behaviour as being 'human' regardless of whether we really approve of it or not. When we start judging people's moral behaviour as being 'inhuman' this is often a good excuse to kill them because we don't like what they are doing. This applies as much to leftists who don't like 'fascist' intolerance as to rightists who don't like self-indulgent permissivism.

D. The Increasing Unity of Humanity

The increasing unity of our concerns for humanity overall. Humanity is more of a self-conscious entity than it ever was in the past. The more we know and understand about what is happening throughout the world, the more we realise how much we have in common. We are more conscious than ever that we all belong to the same species. Everything that is happening in the world conspires to bring us closer together. The credit crisis of 2008 onwards shows us that the affairs of relatively small nations such as Greece can have repercussions for the entire world economy. We belong increasingly to humanity with every concern that we show towards members of our species in far-off parts of the world. Moreover we will only make further progress in getting rid of poverty and inequality by coming ever closer together politically and economically so that every nation on Earth reaches the same level of prosperity. Any political activity that threatens to reduce that unity is to be deplored and denounced.

The very word 'humanity' has grown more important in its meaning and complexity. It is now a unifying focal point for us all since it is a legal term of international significance at least since the Nürnberg trials for crimes against humanity in 1945/46. No nation ill-treating any part of its citizenry can now ignore the concerns of the international community. As a result, during the 20th century a concern for humanity as a whole grew as a focal point bringing all nations together. We now talk about the 'international community' disapproving of or sanctioning this or that nation for its misdeeds. The universal acceptance of human rights and the rule of law throughout the world have brought us closer together in a common system of thought. We all now belong to 'the global village' which unifies us with the complex communications ringing round the world, of which the World Wide Web is only one example.

As a result, wars and disorders throughout the world now concern us all. Such an unprecedented unity of thought and purpose should give us an unparalleled opportunity to put our warring past entirely behind us. The difficulties in achieving this are purely political. There is a lack of strong and visionary political leadership to bring this about. Political leaders are typically inward looking and put their national concerns above all others. Such nationalism ought to be a thing of the past considering how interrelated and bound together we now are as single species. Globalisation is still gathering pace as trade and communications becomes ever more connected and ubiquitous.

Historically, the human race has always been a fractious and divisive species prone to go to war with each other at the drop of a hat. We form ourselves all too easily into opposing tribes whose rivalries all too often descend into violence and war. However, we can now develop a unified world-wide community and break out of that cycle of violence if we put more effort into it than we are at present. The opportunity is there but it may well be missed if the parochial concerns of community, nation and religion are allowed to prevail. The European Union has been showing the way forward even though its future is presently in the balance because of that lingering factionalism and lack of political foresight involving Brexits, Grexits and the like.

The fact is that monoculturalism, not multiculturalism, is the reality now facing us. If we are to avoid the wars, enmities and divisions of the past, then our allegiance to the human race must supersede all other allegiances, lest we forget what we all have in common as human beings. This unifying process transcends multicultural plurality, together with all superficial and ephemeral divisions of nation, race, and religion, to produce a world view common to all humanity. Even racial distinctions are on their way to extinction; a few generations of global intermixture will make racial boundaries impossible to discern. A monoculture is now establishing itself around the world as we become increasingly interlinked by our communications, trade and tourism. Only a strengthening of the global monoculture can ensure the ending of poverty, inequality and injustice which our artificial national and religious divisions can only prolong.

Monoculture does not imply complete uniformity of culture. The institution of a global monoculture does not make human culture exactly the same throughout the globe. The differences between cultures can be based on historical antecedents and not on ideological or religious prejudices that separate cultures from human culture as a whole. The emphasis is on the differences between peoples rather than on nations, races or religions. All the different peoples of the world can be proud of their respective past histories together with their language, literature and the arts while incorporating them in the monoculture of the world. For example, the Scots are proud of their heritage and their cultural peculiarities but these have not prevented Scots from participating fully in British, European and World affairs without losing their Scottish identity. This contrasts, for example, with the historical position of Jewish people who have in the past hived themselves off from any society in which they participated and they suffered the consequences thereof. The Islamic religion is similarly too adept of cutting itself off from other cultures, for example, in its clinging to the retrogressive Shariah law. In contrast, the Scots peopled the world like the Jews but never formed provocative ghettoes that invited pogroms and other atrocities. They were highly individualistic and liked to blend into whatever background in which they found themselves. Similarly, nations such as North Korea that enforce a narrow ideology on their populace become nothing but pariah states ostracised by the international community. Thus, when cultural differences are based on history, language, literature and the arts rather than on ideological or religious dogmatism they can contribute to the global monoculture and not be antipathetic or antagonistic towards it.

Unity of nations makes the collapse of civilisation less likely. As mentioned above, civilisations in the past were localised and confined to specific areas of the globe. They were liable to collapse and disappear, often for internal reasons. However, civilisation now spans the globe and most nations on Earth are now busily adopting the consumer society and finding ways to trade with the rest of the world. It seems unlikely that the world civilisation could collapse entirely as it is increasingly able to absorb localised collapses. It may now be too big to fail because of its increasing size and complexity. The feeble excuse that all civilisations fail in the end simply no longer applies to the great world civilisation now developing before us. The more unified we are as a species the less likely we are to experience decline or extinction.

In summary, therefore, the political will to achieve greater unity is required. Humanity does have a future in so far as we individually and collectively recognise the importance of our unity as a species and make the most of this unity to create a future for ourselves. What is lacking at this time is the vision and political will to aim for greater unity in the future. Hopefully, the holistic view will contribute towards generating that political will.

E. The Need for a Creed

We should understand things before we believe in them. Inevitably what we believe in depends on the culture into which we are born. However, as free individuals, we have the right to think out our beliefs for ourselves, regardless of the beliefs inculcated into us by the dominant culture. This means that we don't succumb to the precepts of tradition or authority without thinking them through for ourselves. Clearly, it is better for us to understand before we believe rather than to believe before understanding. In other words, we find reason within ourselves to arrive at beliefs and don't just believe something simply because we are told that we must believe it. In this way, we give a meaning to our lives that is specifically our own.

As the meaning of our lives lies in what we make of them, we can develop that meaning by drawing on our inner resources. To become responsible for our own beliefs and opinions, we need strength of character sufficient to take on that responsibility. We should be spirited enough to enjoy thinking for themselves. A developed inner being can access our knowledge and experiences as a whole. Compared with this holistic approach, religion has only a therapeutic value in helping people to cope with their lives in the small scale so that they cease to think critically about life as a whole. It is a retrenchment exercise that does not help us to seek truths of value to the future of humanity. In contrast, these truths can be striven for interactively with an open mind. We should look forward to sorting our problems out instead of looking backwardly for divine assistance. Such a human-centred view fosters our positive-mindedness and impels us to get things done rather than dwell dismally on the past. We are concerned to seek the truth and face up to it, however unpleasant or inconvenient it turns out to be. Seeking the truth is not meant to be easy but it can be an exciting and enthralling challenge, provided we have enough depth and breadth of spirit to see it as such. In this way we can keep our minds open to truthful insights.

Our future both as individuals and as a species depends on our believing in ourselves but only in a qualified and self-critical way, in other words, in a self-reflective way. We must constantly examine and re-examine our self-belief so that we can move forward and fulfil our goals and purposes in life. To that end, we need a stable, all-embracing creed based on that self-belief. Without such a creed, we have no standpoint from which to evaluate our actions, aims and purposes. Thus, such a creed can help us to be self-critical instead of forbidding criticism.

A basic creed that we can live by should be practical, sensible and down-to-earth and give us confidence in what we are as mere human beings and in what we can do collectively as a species. It should help us to do things rather than just accept things as they are. We need to think positively about ourselves and our prospects so that we can move on and embrace the future with confidence rather than dwelling on past failings and disappointments.

The characteristics of such a Creed. Thus, the need for a basic and fundamental creed may be fulfilled if it is universal enough to have characteristics such as the following:

- It can be embraced by all believers without necessarily threatening particular beliefs. It will add to these beliefs without undermining them in any way.

- It will go beyond all previous religious creeds while being practical, sensible and down-to-earth. It will not add to the superstitions and implausibilities to which new religions are prone.
- It should give us confidence in what we are as mere human beings and in what we can do collectively as a species. We need to think positively about ourselves and our prospects so that we can move on and embrace the future with confidence rather than dwelling on past failings and disappointments.
- It should therefore help us to do things rather than just accept things as they are. In that respect it will differ from religious creeds which typically promote passivity and obedience.

The Optimist's Creed below goes as far as possible towards fulfilling these conditions. Moreover, it does not expect any more from us than what we normally do in making something of our lives. It involves having faith in ourselves, in humanity and in power of human reason. But this faith needs constant reinforcement by our understanding and criticising what it means and how valid and applicable it is in our daily lives. In that respect, it has a practical and educational role to play rather than a sacred or ritualistic role. For the optimist would rather teach than preach, and not tell people *what* to think but *how* to think. None of the beliefs in this Creed are the whole truth of the matter, but they can help each of us to strive towards the truth in our own way. They are not themselves the way but they attempt to illuminate our way. Thus, the Creed below is a teaching tool designed to help people on their way and not to dictate what that way should be.

The Optimist's Creed helps us in our daily lives to have confidence in our place in the world, in the power of reason, in the value of our fellow human beings, and in value of life in all its varieties. It is meant to be practical and useful. It aims to make sense of matters that will chime with most people. In contrast, religious beliefs, such as a belief in the resurrection of Jesus Christ, or a belief in a paradise awaiting the believers, lack practical application in daily life. Moreover, this Creed is the minimal belief system that can apply to us no matter what other beliefs, religious or non-religious that we may espouse over and above these beliefs. Thus, the faith of an optimist is summed up as follows:

The Optimist's Creed

The Strength of Knowledge

My faith is mightier than mere religion because it is open-ended and founded on ever-increasing knowledge and understanding of what I am, what other people mean to me, and what life and the universe mean to me.

The Power of Critical Reasoning

I have faith in the power of critical reasoning to reach truth, foster goodness, and support justice, and I will conduct a personal quest for all these and will settle for nothing less. I will constantly strive to understand life's mysteries, as far as humanly possible, and will not be content with myths, absurdities, or similar fruitless deviations from truth. I will search for the good within me and within others and will fight for justice and sweet reason for as long as I have the strength and will to do so.

The Capabilities of Humanity

I have faith in the capabilities of humanity, notwithstanding its obvious fallibilities. My belief in its future is not unqualified, as it depends on humanity doing enough to ensure that future. If no one believes in its future then it has no future.

The Resilience of the Human Spirit

I have faith in the resilience and persistence of the human spirit which has already accomplished so much against all the odds. I believe that the spirit within us will prosper for as long as we nurture it and make the most of its potential for good and well-being.

The Uniqueness of Each Individual

I have faith in the potential of every human being to enrich the world with the uniqueness and originality of their contributions to it. I wish to see that uniqueness blossom forth in the right social conditions and thereby justify the existence of humanity.

The Possibilities of Life

I have faith in the possibilities of life which are limited only by the paucity of human imagination. I believe that life has secure foundations while the human race believes in itself and its mission to further life. This requires each of us to make the most of our lives within the limits of our unique potential. In so doing, we serve the purposes of life as much as we are the custodians of it.

Finally, humanity is like a ship at sea forever repairing itself as it sails along without hope of reaching dry land where more complete and effective repairs can be made. In other words, we are a self-sustaining, self-justifying species, which must rely on its own resources and ingenuity, and can expect no external help in its endeavours. This isolation gives us opportunities and challenges that we cannot shun without dishonouring ourselves. And there is no need for us to invent friendly, helpful entities of whose existence there is no convincing evidence. If we have enough confidence in ourselves then we can do without them. When we take responsibility for our own future, they become superfluous and subject to Occam's razor.

6. Science - Expanding the Middle Ground

A. Science and the Middle Ground

We are all scientific-minded in our desire for knowledge of some kind or other. We become scientists in the broadest sense of the word when we acquire knowledge that enables us to do worthwhile things in the world. Science in this sense includes skills and practical know-how as well as the theoretical knowledge provided by the physical and social sciences. Knowing what science is and what it can do for us is essential to our complete development as human beings. Unless we understand what science is telling us, we can never understand ourselves, society or the universe. This, an unscientific education is an incomplete one since science helps us to understand our strengths and weaknesses both as individuals and as a species.

The holistic view imbibes scientific knowledge as a means of relating to the universe and its contents. It is one of the ways that we face up to the realities of life and living. This does not mean acquiring detailed scientific knowledge but understanding the important role that such knowledge plays in establishing our place in the universe. That knowledge consists in expanding the middle ground between the very small and the very large. It is constantly adding to our knowledge of our surroundings from the smallest to the largest and everything in between.

Through physics we get insight into the quantum realms and through astronomy we reach out to the ends of the universe. Between these extremes, we have sciences such as biology, zoology and the social sciences such as economics and psychology. By expanding the area of this middle ground, science helps us to consolidate our position in the universe. Our importance to the universe grows in proportion to the growth of our understanding of it. In exploring the universe from the centre outwards, we understand better our role in the universe according to what science is telling us. We get, for example, an increasing understanding of how we have emerged quite naturally from the complexifying processes inherent in the universe. Life has made itself without having to be made by anything else. In facing such realities we find the middle ground between thinking too much of ourselves and too little. We reach a more balanced state of understanding our place as opposed to an overweening pride at one extreme and a self-deprecating humility at the other extreme.

Our natural curiosity drives us to understand what we are and what our role in the universe is. If we are interested in science in general then we are scientists in the widest sense of the word. We all have the potential to understand and use science. It doesn't matter whether or not we actually contribute to scientific knowledge. It is enough to study science and to understand it even at a general or populist level. Such a study opens our minds to the possibilities of further scientific understanding. The receptivity and ability to retain one's curiosity and open-mindedness are all important.

Scientific knowledge is important from a holistic point of view in helping us understand our middle position between the immensely large and immensely small things in the universe. The more we understand about that middle position, the more we secure our position in the universe and feel more secure within ourselves. To share in the security of this greater knowledge and understanding we must all act as scientists who use scientific knowledge about ourselves and the universe we live in, to the best of our personal abilities.

By including everything from the very small to the very large, science brings together everything about energy, matter, life and humanity. This includes the sciences of life and humanity, namely, biology, zoology as well as sociology, psychology and economics. Each science is engaged to a greater or lesser extent in relating the very small to the very large and *vice versa*. For example, medical science looks at microbes as well as elephants. Economics relates the behaviour of individual consumers to the economy as a whole and ultimately to the global economy as a whole. (As we all know to our cost, it cannot yet predict anything with scientific accuracy or reliability.) Physics gives us quantum mechanics as well as the rocket science to reach the planets and hopefully the stars.

The Infinitely Large and Infinitely Small. Another way of putting it is that we are placed the finite middle between what is potentially infinitely large and infinitely small. Infinity stretches from us in all directions both inside us and outside us. In that sense, humanity is indeed at the centre of the universe. When we take a purely physical view of humanity, it is clear on the large scale that we are physically insignificant to the nth degree. Many people despair of their existence when it strikes them hard just how insignificant we appear to be in that context. It is too easy to think that humanity is worthless in the face of the universe's unfathomable immensity. Yet that is only one perspective. The same facts show our true importance in the universe when we consider our hugeness compared with very small things such as cells and atoms. We are both infinitely small and infinitely large at the same time. This can be simply illustrated by putting one's forefinger and thumb together and then separate them by a tiny gap. The Earth is far smaller than that gap in relation to the size of the Milky Way galaxy, and the latter is just as small compared to the rest of the universe. At the same time, the cells in our body are far smaller than that gap, and atoms are as small in relation to the cells as the latter are to us. Though we are rendered miniscule by the hugeness of the universe, we are also rendered massive compared with the extreme tininess of cells, molecules, atoms, quarks and so on.

B. The Role of the Middle View

The middle view is important because it confirms our role at the centre of the universe. It enables us to revive the pre-Copernican view of humanity as being at the centre of the universe. This bolsters our self-belief and gives us good reasons for having this self-belief. Above all, we need it if we are to take responsibility for our own future as a species. We have to believe in ourselves because nothing else will. As is already argued above, self-belief is all important. It is a matter of finding reasons for that self-belief. Positive reasons are just as valid and truthful as negative ones. It all depends how the evidence is interpreted and from what viewpoint. Ever since Copernicus displaced the Earth from the centre of the universe, astronomy has increasingly revealed the immensity of our insignificance. We have lost a great deal of faith in ourselves as a result of these discoveries. But this view is all in the mind. We can interpret the facts from a different viewpoint that changes our minds about our position in the universe. Being in a mid-position between the extremely large and extremely small is just the change of mind being proposed here

Everything we now know about the universe indicates that humanity has no future unless it makes its own future. We stand alone in this infinitesimally tiny part of the universe and must make the best of our isolation unless and until we find other intelligent life-forms elsewhere in the universe. We will then have a better idea of our true significance in the universe. In the meantime we can find within ourselves sufficient reasons to consider us to be important in the universe, particularly as regards our middle position therein. We are not at the centre of the universe in the sense that it does not revolve around us and that we are incredibly small in relation to its enormity. But there are other senses in which we are at the centre of things, especially in our being in a middle position between the very large and the very small, as is argued further below.

The Copernican view is one-sided and incomplete. It provides us with only one perspective that is not the necessary or absolute truth of the matter. It does not encompass everything that we can understand from the available facts. From other perspectives we can think of ourselves as being at the heart of the universe. We are to ourselves is just as important as we are in purely physical terms. This has always been the religious view as against the scientific view of things. But religion is incompatible with science in demanding absolute and unqualified faith or belief in its tenets.

It gives us a broad view of our potential as, for example, our being made in the image of God, at the price of narrowing our minds to one dogmatic system or another. But this view is not broad enough. Religion no longer provides good enough answers to account for our place in the universe as God has been made increasingly irrelevant by the scientific facts. We must now find the strength within ourselves to make our own way forward (hence the title of my first book, *The Answers Lie Within Us*). In place of the extreme religious and scientific standpoints, this book offers a holistic, human-centred viewpoint that omits the irrelevancies and superfluities on which religious belief depends, while at the same time taking matters of belief more seriously than the scientific view usually does.

We can now reinstate to some extent a pre-Copernican view of humanity in which we are more important to the universe than our insignificant material existence suggests. This returns us to our rightful place at the heart and centre of the universe. We belong there because we know what we are as a species, and what we have and have not accomplished, for better or for worse. We belong there because nothing else that we know of can adopt such a place or make anything of it. Thus, our self-knowledge alone puts us at the heart of the universe.

We are worthy of such a position because we know enough about ourselves to take responsibility for our own actions and to establish our own place in the universe. We may fail to do so through lack of vision and self-seeking short-termism. However, we are potentially self-critical enough to know all about the mistakes that we have been making, about our ineffectiveness as a species, and about the very limited things we can do in this vast universe. That knowledge is itself an accomplishment. It allows us to be self-reliant and no longer to rely on the sanction and discipline of external beings whose existence is not manifest. The human race should now regard itself as grown up enough to make its own way forward without the support of such fictitious entities.

We are important because our presence cannot be denied or refuted, even though as bits of matter we are vanishingly small and next to nothing. Thus, our presence here and now makes us important. The meaningfulness and purposefulness of our thoughts and actions gives us a presence that transcends our material existence. When we believe in the importance of our presence here and now, then we are important because the belief alone creates the fact, which does not exist without our contemplating it. We are no more important than what we believe ourselves to be, as long as our beliefs are based on the established facts of our existence and the hard realities of life and living.

This is not a matter of believing in ourselves religiously, absolutely or unrealistically. Our limitations are made plain enough in a self-critical open society that does not allow us to get beyond ourselves. Our self-belief is self-regulatory and entirely dependent on ourselves. Mass media scrutiny supplies the self-regulatory mechanisms required to criticise and monitor our activities and keep us on the right track. For example, our awareness of the parlous state of our environment arouses passions in its defence. As a result, lobbying organisations such as Friends of the Earth and Greenpeace actively ensure that governments and big business cannot overlook the environmental effects of our activities. Their activities make no sense unless they are assuming that a better state of affairs can be arrived at in which we have more balanced and rational relationship with the rest of the planet. In other words, they implicitly believe that humanity has a future worthy of itself and its place in the scheme of things.

C. The Centrality of our Position in the Universe

Science tells us we are the middle species. The truth about our importance lies in examining exactly what science tells us our place in the universe. We are indeed insignificantly small in relation to the universe at large. But we are in our turn are immensely large in relation to the miniscule atomic sphere of existence. We are a middle species that lies between the imaginably large and the inconceivably small areas of existence. These facts cannot be emphasised or repeated enough. The following details are adapted from freely available internet information and demonstrate the extent to which this is the ultimate truth of the matter.

We are immensely small	*We are immensely large*
The true scale of our physical insignificance seems scarcely imaginable. Yet we can imagine this insignificance to some extent. The Earth is not much bigger than pinhead from the distance at which the sun is positioned. But then the whole solar system is even smaller than a pinhead in relation to the Milky Way galaxy of which it forms a part. Then our galaxy appears to be no more than a pinhead from far outside it. And there are millions upon millions of other similar tiny galaxies in the universe. We are infinitely small within infinitely small pinheads. We are therefore the tiniest of the tiny within the tiniest of tiny.	We tower over very small things as much as very large things tower over us. Thus, the cells in our bodies are invisibly small. At least a thousand human cells would fit into a grain of sand measuring a millimetre in length. There are about 100 trillion cells in the average human body. Yet each cell is a mini-factory doing thousands of jobs such as synthesising proteins, deposing of waste products, and making enzymes and hormones to serve the body's needs. We have no conscious control over the workings of individual cells as their functioning is entirely automatic. We may physically dominate these tiny cells but we are nothing without them

Our cosmic insignificance is even greater when we consider the numbers involved. The Milky Way galaxy contains some 200–400 billion stars, of which the Sun is an insignificant one placed the edge of a spiral arm. The galaxy is estimated to contain 50 billion planets, 500 million of which could be located in the habitable zone of their parent star. It is roughly 100,000 light years in diameter, and our nearest sister galaxy, the Andromeda Galaxy, is located roughly 2.5 million light years away. (Each light year is approximately 5.8 trillion miles in length.) There are probably more than 100 billion (10^{11}) galaxies in the observable universe. Typical galaxies range from dwarfs with as few as ten million (10^7) stars up to giants with one trillion (10^{12}) stars, all orbiting the galaxy's centre of mass. A 2010 study by astronomers estimated that the observable universe contains 300 sextillion (3×10^{23}) stars. The chances of intelligent life being on the planets revolving round some of these must be quite high.

We are huge in relation to our cells but the latter are huge in relation of the atoms of which they are composed. Within each human cell there are as much as 200 trillion atoms. (That makes 200 septillion atoms in each human body – 2 followed by 24 zeros! There are more atoms in our bodies than stars are estimated to be in the universe - 300 sextillion.) Each atom is mainly empty space. If an atom were the size of a cathedral, its nucleus would be the size of a fly at the centre of it. The rest of the space is empty apart from electrons zooming around. These electrons repel those of other atoms and keep them apart. Electrons cannot be predicted to be anywhere in particular. At these levels of existence, the automatic functioning that we see in cells breaks down. Electrons, photons and other tiny atomic particles can never be pinned down. Whatever we do to them changes their position and even whether they are particles or waves. Chance and uncertainty reign at the lowest levels accessible to us.

D. The Importance of our Centrality

Our middle position gives us knowledge in both directions. The fact that we are both big and small helps us to understand how living beings on the surface of this ridiculously small lump of rock can know so much about themselves. How can we possibly know the extent of our physical insignificance but also something of the workings of the universe as a whole? The answer must lie in the fact that our physical insignificance is only one half of the story. Our insignificance must be balanced with our immensity in size in the other direction. We are really at the half-way house in the scheme of things. If we go in the other direction, we find that everything gets just as remotely small and as the universe is remotely large. Our centrality enables us to take equal account of both directions.

What is going on far below the level of our sight is truly wondrous and is not without purpose. When we think of immensely small cells as tiny factories that are reliably productive throughout our lives, we can't help but be amazed at what life achieves at these levels. Life does all these things on its own without external assistance. Also, we now know that the air is full of equally small bacteria that populate the Earth to a far greater extent than we will ever achieve. The fact that we are increasingly aware of the power of life at these levels makes us important custodians of life. Our undoubted role is to mediate between these extremes and make sure that life gets and keeps a firm footing in the universe. The fact that we can think of adopting such a role means that we are honour bound to take it up. Not to do so would be an abnegation of our very existence as self-styled intelligent beings; we would rightly shame ourselves in the eyes of posterity. People in the future will think us very stupid indeed, if we do not have the confidence and responsibility to make the most of our custodial role on Earth.

Beyond doubt, science helps us to relate the very small to the very large and thereby bring order, meaning and purpose into being that did not exist previously. We create order by linking the very large with the very small and making a coherent system of them. We are already doing this with a significant measure of success with the sciences of cosmology, physics, chemistry, biology and the other sciences. The purpose of the experiments at CERN and other research centres is to help us understand how the behaviour of immensely small nuclear particles relates to how the universe at large came into existence, what it is composed of, and what is happening to it, now and in the future. At these small levels it appears that everything is connected with everything else and whatever happens there has implications for the universe as a whole. Thus, to understand the beginnings of the universe and how it is expanding, it is necessary to understand how things function at the very smallest level of existence.

Everything is physically *determined* at the very large level of existence and everything is physically *undetermined* at the very smallest level of existence. It is only at our middle level of existence that freedom of thought and movement becomes possible; everything else is subject to chance or necessity. Thus, freedom is only ensured at our middle position. However, to say that we have such freedom is itself a middle position between the extreme views of the sceptic and the determinist. A sceptic typically argues that we are subject to chance events over which we have no control, and the determinist holds that we have no freedom from necessarily determined events. But most of us prefer to believe that we have some freedom in our thoughts and acts. We believe that we can freely choose between alternative courses of actions.

We can also freely choose to make something or nothing of the universe. Our importance in the universe lies in our middle position which enables us to think and act for ourselves in ways that are not possible at the very large or very small levels of existence. Our freedom to think and act enables us to understand what is happening at the very large and very small levels of existence. We are the key to understanding the universe. Our place in the universe enables us to gain some understanding of the interconnections at the very largest and very smallest levels of existence. Understanding fully our true status in the universe therefore depends on our increasing knowledge of what is happening at both these levels. By our unstinting efforts we can make something of the universe. In contrast, we are also free to do nothing at all and therefore make no mark on the universe whatsoever. This has often been the religious position down the ages.

If it were possible for God to exist somewhere in the universe, it could only be found at the middle position. Only at that position can the notion of God be contemplated with any meaning. Our middle position shows us that nothing having creative or purposeful capabilities can exist in the direction of either the very large or the very small. At these extremes there is nothing but determinacy or indeterminacy; necessity or chance. There is no possibility of any sentient entity existing at these extremes, let alone an omnipotent, omniscient or omnipresent being. Moreover, the universe began as an infinitely small point and to increase our understanding of its beginning we need to research into that extremely small area of existence. It can only be understood better in this way by intelligent beings operating at the middle position. Thus, as intelligence is only to be found at the middle position, beings superior to ourselves will only be found at that position. Until we make the first contact with such beings, we can confidently say that God does not exist at present and that we are the only hope of god-like beings coming into existence in the future by our becoming extremely advanced beings with divine powers of our own.

Our quest for knowledge is an investment in the future. Thus, future knowledge can save us from denigrating ourselves to total insignificance. We must invest in the future in that regard by supporting whatever expensive research is required to gain greater understanding of the universe both at the macroscopic and microscopic levels. Cosmological understanding is linked at a very deep level with quantum understanding, since the universe began at that infinitely small level of existence. Indeed, the very fact that we can conduct such research and gain an astonishing amount of information about the universe, near and far, shows that we are unique in being able to do so. No other species on Earth has come close to such achievements, and no other species can be relied upon to do so in the near future. Therein lies our ultimate importance as a species.

In conclusion, we can use our centrality to benefit ourselves, life, the cosmos and posterity. We are at the interface between the very large and the very small, and it is here that we can (1) establish our value in the universe, (2) find meaning in all that we do or do not do in the world, and (3) form the purposes that make sense of our lives. At this position we can mediate between all other forms of life, both big and small. By putting them all in their place and valuing them all accordingly, we ascribe cosmic significance to all life-forms as well as ourselves. Also, at this intermediary position, increasing order and beauty are created not only by us but also by other intelligent beings, assuming they exist in the universe. As a result, the Cosmos is created which is the increasing orderliness that will possibly save the universe from its ultimate fate of total dispersal and heat death. Finally, by using our insights, knowledge and abilities in a meaningful and purposeful way, we leave a legacy to posterity which will be to their benefit and which will be an example that they can build on to take humanity forward.

7. Art - Eternalising our Creativity

A. The Way to Artistic Achievement

In the widest sense, we are all artists who can be creative one way or another. We can all benefit holistically by making the most of our potential artistry. As artists, we can dream up what has never been thought or created before. By putting our dreams into practice, we give them a concrete existence that can last for as long as their materiality persists. Thus, our artistic role is to bring new things into being that will be long-lasting and ultimately eternal.

Our dreams may be beneficial or destructive. The destructive ones diminish us while the beneficial ones can inspire and enthuse us. Dreams about killing people and destroying things can do us no credit unless we can use them in beneficial way in our artistic creations. The nightmarish paintings of Hieronymus Bosch are obvious examples of negativity being transformed into positive art. The positive approach is therefore one element in ensuring the durability of our artistic contributions.

In seeking to eternalise art, it is necessary to get the creative process right. Art is characteristically intuitive in its origins but its application requires the use of reason and intelligence. The creative process might be described as follows. An idea occurs to us intuitively and by the skilful use of reason and intelligence a work of art is produced. We use our brains to bring an artistic insight into practical reality. Thus, both creativity and intelligence are both involved in the artistic process. The interrelationship between intelligence and creativity is extremely important and this interrelationship is rudimentarily shown in the following diagram:

$$\text{Intelligence} \leftrightarrows \text{Creativity}$$
$$\downarrow \qquad\qquad \downarrow$$
$$\text{Reason} \leftrightarrows \text{Intuition}$$
$$\downarrow \qquad\qquad \downarrow$$
$$\text{Understanding} \leftrightarrows \text{Aesthetic Feelings}$$
$$\searrow \qquad \swarrow$$
$$\searrow \qquad \swarrow$$

contributing to

Artistic Achievement

The interactions of reason/intuition and understanding/aesthetics feelings are crucial to the artistic process. They are implied when the painter uses his intelligence and creativity, for example, when he judges whether his painting is as beautiful and striking as he wants it to be. The importance of these distinctions lies in their interrelationships with each other. The one feeds off the other since by becoming more intelligent we increase our creative potential and *vice versa.* Our intellectual abilities are enhanced by our artistic bent, and our artistic inclinations are given sense and purpose by our intellectual interests. For example, an inventor would get nowhere with his intuitive ideas unless he works out intelligently how the public might benefit from his ideas and how to get them to the production level to sell them to the public. The interaction between creativity and intelligence is important not only to the artistic process but also to humanity in general. It is therefore worth considering in more depth.

B. The Role of Creativity and Intelligence

Intelligence and creativity are important to the holistic view in general, and they are also vital to our future. Unless we use them to make a better future for ourselves, we don't deserve it. Intelligent and creative behaviour is resonant of sagacity, insight and foresight. It is intelligent behaviour not to do things that are unworthy of us. It is creative behaviour to find new and different ways of doing things that are productive and worthwhile doing in themselves. Thus, in this context, being intelligent means being thoughtful and considerate, and being creative means rethinking things anew. The one is reasonable and the other intuitive, and we need both if we are to be wise and well-rounded individuals.

It is not enough for us to be intelligent and creative individuals, we need also to be intelligent and creative as a species. The lack of intelligence and creativity ever threatens our future. It is not intelligent to maintain confrontational nation states forever ready to go to war with each other. It is not intelligent to misuse our creativity in creating more efficient weapons to kill each other. The more we make the best possible use of our intelligence and creativity, the more we can justify our existence and make sense of our lives. In applying them as individuals we can become wise and worthy people who make all the difference in the world. Making the most of these attributes brings us all together as human beings whatever we believe or do not believe. Intelligence and creativity are therefore the *leitmotifs* or recurring themes that dominate the thinking behind the holistic view

Intelligence and creativity shows itself to be so in what we do or don't do in our daily lives. We show our intelligence in the actions that are shown to be effective and appropriate and are generally accepted to be such by those witnessing and benefiting from them. Similarly, creativity involves introducing something new and different which is shown to be so and is generally accepted to be so by those who appreciate it as it being an example of creativity in action. Thus, intelligent and creative behaviour is judged to be so by the general acceptance of independent communities of inquirers, critics or participants who are interested enough to pass judgment. The ultimate community is of course that of public opinion, whether it is or is not manipulated by the mass media.

Intelligence is inextricably entwined with creativity and *vice versa*, so that the interrelationship between them is crucial. An intelligent act can be seen to be creative in some way, and a creative act involves intelligence in some way. Our mastery of computers involves a series of intelligent acts that are often creative in that we may not have thought of them before. Computers constantly give us problems of which we have had no previous experience. By our ingenuity we can often overcome these problems without consulting helplines and the like. In thinking things out for ourselves, we do things differently and therefore creatively. Indeed, our most commonplace actions give us scope for creativity by finding new and different ways of doing things. Ideally, we can all benefit when every one uses intelligence and creativity to the best of their abilities. Equally, we all benefit from living in an intelligent and creative community. These are social ideals that we must constantly strive for, even though we often fall short of attaining them. They result in the one benefiting the many. This is the crucial interaction between the one and the many that makes all social cultures work, for example, those of the ants and bees.

In summary, therefore, it is important to use our intelligence creatively. Intelligence in this context refers to our rational side while creativity takes in our intuitive side. In our quest for truth and knowledge we use our intelligence, and in finding beauty and feeling in all things our creativity is stimulated. Intelligence depends on reason and knowledge that are based on truth, while creativity is inspired by beauty and other intuitions that impact on our senses and inner feelings. We need to make the most of these to living life to the full. However, the argument is that intelligence and creativity are not sufficient by themselves to bring about wisdom. They need to go through the mill that involves learning all the roles of the holistic viewpoint. As human beings we are partly rational and partly intuitive. Intelligence involves being rational and creativity thrives on intuition. Wisdom consists in combining the both of these without going to one extreme or the other.

Intelligence and creativity are beyond doubt the most important things in the universe, which is otherwise a dull place full of meaningless stupidities unless we counter these by behaving intelligently and doing creative things. We human beings can consider ourselves important to the universe in the valuable things we bring into being that would not exist otherwise, especially creative objects and ideas. When we brighten it up for ourselves, it is a brighter place in itself. Our value lies in the new and different things we introduce into it that did not exist before. Our knowledge and our art shine forth despite all our flaws and faults. The universe progresses from dull uniformity to dazzling diversity, and we contribute to that process in ways never hitherto countenanced. We belong to the universe as we are a part of its natural processes in becoming more diverse and different as it expands and develops.

Holism therefore emphasises our oneness with the universe, as we are indeed children of the universe. That human beings live at all is such a fortuitous event that we owe a debt of gratitude to the universe which has given rise to us against all the odds. If it were configured differently we would not have existed in any shape or form. Events in the past could have turned out so very differently. We are indebted because we live and the alternative to life is to be nothing at all. We can repay that debt by using our intelligence and creativity to add to its diversity.

That we exist at all as human beings is an important fact in itself. Every human being is capable of displaying intelligence of some sort and of creating things that did not exist before. We vindicate our existence by the intelligent and creative things we do, and the holistic view helps us to make the most of ourselves with a better future in mind. Our being and doing makes us important in the universe. We are at the cutting edge of the universe; we are the scythe by which universe cuts its way to the future. Nothing else can achieve this. Only by using out intelligence and creativity can we achieve a better and richer future which we bequeath to the universe in living our whole lives to that end.

Intelligence and creativity are always in need of active promotion and approbation, as we can never really be intelligent or creative enough. Even the most handicapped and challenged human being has intelligence and creativity to contribute to the whole. Everyone has intellectual potential of some sort. For example, the physicist Stephen Hawking is as handicapped as anyone can be but he is still making valuable contributions to human life and learning. Thus, everyone is capable of achieving wisdom by using their intelligence and creativity to the best of their abilities and for the best of reasons. Every child born on Earth has potential beyond the wildest dreams of its parents. The faults and failings of its parents need not prevent it from its fulfilling its potential. The blame lies more with the necessarily limited nature of society into which the child is born. None of us can become any more than our society is capable of enabling us to become. We are all born into a society that is limited in its growth and development. It can only go a very small way towards helping us to fulfil our potential. It is up to us as individuals to stretch society further and ensure its further development so that everyone benefits from it.

C. Taking Account of Eternity

There is no end to the artist's vision and ingenuity. It stretches nigh to eternity. Thus, there is a touch of the eternal in the artist's intelligence and creativity that takes them beyond the commonplace here and now. The very idea of eternity is important for artists as it broadens their thinking about things. It takes their artistic achievements into a higher context. Every creative act brings about changes that change things forever. Moreover, beauty in whatever form is forever. So the artist's works are eternalised in their very creativity. His standpoint must be *sub specie aeternitatis* - under the aspect of eternity.

The word 'eternity' is nothing more than a notion or concept that exists in the mind but nevertheless it helps us to make sense of the universe we inhabit. It refers to the everlastingness of things; the possibility that things can go on forever and ever. This is useful because it is within the aspect and prospect of eternity that we can embrace everything that will possibly take us forward to the future. It includes everything concerning us that lasts without end and stretches to infinity. It is the sphere of the sublime that surpasses all. We broaden our minds and stretch our imaginations beyond everyday life in contemplation of the eternal. We transcend the middle ground to trawl our imaginations concerning what has not come into being and what is beyond all present being. It underlines the all-encompassing view of the artist in contributing things of awe and beauty. The view of eternity is therefore that of glimpsing the eternal and embracing it as a viewpoint. It is the view of the Muses of old, and is therefore that of the artist or creative person of whatever description.

In eternity, the Platonic forms take their ultimate place though that place is only in our thinking about things. Though eternity embraces the everlasting nature of Platonic forms, it does not confirm their reality. These forms do not exist outside the categories that we impose on the world. Their place is therefore in our minds. Truth and beauty reside there and the artist accesses to them in their transcendent form. The artist is therefore tasked with bringing the eternal view out-of-mind and down-to-earth by representing it in a material form which may be artistic, literary, visual or whatever the imagination of the artist can conjure up. Thus, in holistic view, the artist is the sublime exponent of eternal forms.

The eternal view is therefore essential to the artist as it looks at things from afar and gives a long-lasting standpoint from which to judge works of art. In so far as 'eternal' means lasting forever and ever, all existence lies before the artist and all feelings related to that existence. The artist uses the present to put the past together with its future prospects in mind. This millenarian attitude expands our minds to infinity. In every painting, poem, symphony or other work of art there must be a universal theme otherwise there is nothing in it to appeal to the bulk of those viewing, reading or listening to their works. The artist at his best seeks truth and beauty in his works of art and these ensure their eternal significance. In being creative, artists are more prospective than retrospective in their outlook. They are looking forward to new and different things that will make the future different from the past. The eternal view of the artist therefore includes the ability to look to the future and anticipate the needs of future generations. This is important because our value as artists is ultimately judged by posterity.

However, it is important to note that eternity is not God. In religion, eternity is often equated with God who is portrayed as an everlasting being compared with temporality of the human being. God is also thought to be a perfect being. But both eternity and perfection are mere ideas that exist only to order our thinking about the universe and our place in it. The notion of eternity helps us to expand our thinking beyond the temporal existence to which we are condemned throughout our lives. Ir is an inherently human thing with no divine attributes beyond our own divine aspirations.

We can speculate that everything and nothing is preserved within the scope of eternity. At the moment of death we enter eternity and then everything is nothing to us. We come out of the eternal nothingness at birth and re-enter it at death. Between these two empty instances, our lives are lived and they potentially persist for eternity since there is nothing else in it. The eternal existence of things perhaps belongs within the zero point field postulated by physicists. Our lives may be accessible there for an eternity. All the thoughts and images that pass through our minds are looped into this field wherein their existence is guaranteed in some way at present unaccountable to us. These at least survive us for an eternity even though our lives have come to a predictable end. It is not beyond the bounds of possibility that eternity is perennially accessible at that level of existence.

8. Cosmos - Developing the Holistic View

A. The Role of the Cosmos

The notion of Cosmos embodies the holistic view. It is used to bring everything together that is significant about us. All our holistic roles merge into contributions to the Cosmos. What we do as vitalist, illuminists, moralists, humanists, optimists, scientists and artists can add to the Cosmos. It is what we are, whereas the eternal is ever beyond us. The artistic view is limited by what is creatively eternal. The artist's vision goes beyond the mere human and is abstract in the extreme. But it is not the completely all-embracing view since it stands outside human affairs. It is only focused on creative contributions that potentially last forever. From a strictly human point of view, what is important about any artistic achievement is the extent of its cosmic contribution. In that way, it contributes to the holistic view which goes beyond the artistic view in taking in everything to do with humanity. It is ultimately what is here called the cosmic view.

The Cosmos encompasses not only everything that we know about the material universe but also everything that the human race has brought into being through its cultural endeavours, both mental and physical. It is not God but is only symbolic of what humanity is and has achieved. Just as the knowledge contained in Wikipedia is imposed on no one, so the Cosmos demands nothing of anyone. Like Wikipedia, it is there to be used and contributed to. However, it goes far beyond that incomparable encyclopaedia in containing it and everything else achieved by and attributable to humanity. In this way, the cosmist can appreciate all and everything about humanity however adverse he may be to particular aspects of it.

The cosmist is also a holist since taking things as a whole means embracing all that humanity has to offer – past, present and future. The cosmist's role is to bestow value on all our achievements and proclaim their meaning and importance to all and sundry. Wholeness implies completeness and what lasts forever is only a part of the whole. What is being done in the here and now is also included. Thus, the Cosmos is the imaginary repository by which holists carry around not so much all knowledge in their heads but the appreciation and applicability of it. That knowledge is always accessible online, in books, videos and the heads of experts but it is useless unless it is appreciated and applied whenever the occasion arises by those who see when and where it is needed. The cosmist is therefore a visionary who takes account of all that humanity has to offer and makes as much of it as his imagination will allow.

As a mere carry-all, the Cosmos is not to be worshipped or adulated since it is merely a notion that serves to put the whole of humanity in the broadest possible perspective. Only we as human beings can do this and not any imaginary beings that are only invented by reflecting on our own capabilities or the lack of them. If we are wise, we will try our best to embrace everything without exception in our thoughts and images. Though we may never attain this completely or perhaps only temporarily, we can't stop trying. To stop trying is to start dying. Life gives us no choice if we want to carry on living.

The ultimate nature of the Cosmos. The Cosmos gives us the remote view of humanity that we need to appreciate its ultimate value and significance, and it is an important object of holist's view to absorb and develop that viewpoint. As herein defined, it is the *ne plus ultra* view of what we are and the place we have in it. It gives us a humane way of measuring and judging our achievements objectively without having to resort to a divine perspective that is really unfathomable and beyond our ken.

Nevertheless, the Cosmos cannot include absolutely everything. It is a human notion devoted to human concerns. For example, it does not include posterity. Future generations can only be imagined to exist as the legacy of our present efforts. The Cosmos points to the future which we are constantly working towards in our daily lives. It is emblematic of everything we have achieved as a species. Our future is not in making intelligent robots that would make humanity extinct. It is in building up a Cosmos which can perhaps be launched from Earth and reach the furthest corners of the universe. Doubtless, we will do this as soon as move off this planet and spread ourselves and life across the universe. Robots will be helpful to that end which may be their ultimate function and not that of replacing us. Thus, building up the Cosmos is a prelude to our making our lasting mark on the universe.

Moreover, we move forward as a species when we take account of everything that we have achieved and strive to contribute further to our past achievements. The all-embracing view of the Cosmos is crucial to our progress whether we attain it completely or not. Everything about humanity and its achievements is gathered together in this broad notion of the Cosmos. It contains not just the internet but everything else that we have done in creating buildings, bridges, works of art, and so on, as is listed below. It is therefore the ultimate expression of humanity and everything about it. It is the converse of being divine or religious, as it is literally ourselves writ large. The notion helps us to bring ourselves into perspective and to see our Cosmic importance instead of belittling ourselves purposelessly as religion tends to do. The act of thinking about humanity and our achievements adds to its importance and strengthens our view of ourselves. This encourages us to do all that is necessary to advance humanity and life in general. In short, we see our contributions to humanity as being more meaningful and purposeful when they are put into this broad Cosmic context.

Our Cosmic position. In the vastness of space, which is otherwise composed of mindless matter and energy, something different is being constructed on our minuscule planet. It is a tiny seed of unifying harmony and order that we are bringing into being in exercising our intelligence and creativity in a reasonable, responsible and purposeful way. This is here called the 'Cosmos' which in conceptual terms we can contrast with the material universe. The universe is gradually being blasted to fragments but at the heart of it we, together with all living beings, are unifying agents who are countering this relentless dissipation of matter and energy. Living beings complexify matter and thereby bring meaning and purpose into the universe that is otherwise meaningless and purposeless. We, the human race, are doing more in creating this Cosmic unifying entity. The Cosmos brings together the additional meaning and purpose that we are contributing with our peculiar intelligence and creativity. This Cosmos is like a seed that will sprout forth in the far future though exactly what form it will ultimately take we can scarcely image. We might think of it as a god in the making. But it is not god now; it is only us making something of ourselves when we act intelligently and creatively.

The Cosmos is a part of the universe because we are a part of the universe. But it is distinct from it in being centred on ourselves and other intelligent beings capable of contributing to it. The universe is the external reality with which we interact to make our mark on it. What we do in the universe brings the Cosmos into being as something unique to ourselves. Thus, we can differentiate the notion of the Cosmos from the universe to draw attention to human achievements in a universe in which we otherwise appear to be infinitesimally small compared with its unimaginably size.

The Cosmos is more than just imaginary as it is confirmed by the evidence of human activity in all fields including the arts, music, and literature. That activity is real enough in that it produces concrete products that cannot be overlooked – buildings, books, artworks and so on. The Cosmos embraces everything that has happened to us in the past and is happening to us in the present. Its persistence is confirmed by the eternal existence of the past and of everything that has happened in the past. The everlasting Cosmos may be differentiated from the universe as containing everything that exists forever, whereas the universe continues to move on into the future and to disintegrate entropically. The differences between the universe and the cosmos may be summed up as follows:

UNIVERSE	COSMOS
Lacking Meaning and Purpose	Gathering Meaning and Purpose
Decaying Matter	Organising Order
Ultimately Destructive	Creatively Constructive
Impersonal and Quantifiable	Personal and Qualitative
Decaying into the Future	Accumulating all for the Future
Indifferent to us	Expressive of us

The notion of Cosmos is needed to bring together everything about us that is more than just matter and energy. It goes beyond the internet and all the intercommunications that make up human society. In this context, it includes all our physical creations as well as those in literature, science, art, music, commerce, industry and the rest. All our buildings, bridges, artefacts, infrastructure, even our gardens and parks may be included in the all-encompassing bracket of contributions to the Cosmos. It is in a sense a divine being in the making in that it refers to everything 'divine' and 'sacred' about us, namely, when our activities and achievements amount to something more than the sum total of its parts and are valued in more than just material or financial terms. It is gradually building towards a god-like status in the far future. At present, the Cosmos is not God in any sense of the word, but it is a way of moving slowly and modestly towards what we conceive to be a more divine state of affairs than what exists at the present time. It gives direction to our culture and civilisation. We and all intelligent beings who know their place in the universe are together in bringing into existence something that embodies everything intelligent and creative about us.

Everything that we value in life belongs to the Cosmos and not to the decaying material universe. Whatever we do on this planet makes no difference to the universe at large. The universe is indifferent to our very existence. But what we do is of great importance to the Cosmos since its very existence depends on us and what we do with our lives. It is a notion by which we objectify ourselves and all our doings. It is what we are and what we do writ large so that we can interrelate with it as if it were distinct from us. We can relate to it because it is what we *are* basically as a productive, intelligent, creative species. We relate to it abstractly and it refers back to us at this abstract level of existence. It is an interactive notion which exists in our minds but which takes us out of ourselves in a positive way. We can view ourselves objectively and assess our achievements through this notion of the Cosmos. It is more than an object of imagination or fantasy since we can use it to evaluate ourselves and what we are doing. It gives us a goal to aim for, namely, that of developing and enriching the Cosmos. Its existence is qualitative and therefore aspirational. We aspire to it as being representative of the best we are capable of achieving with and in our lives.

In making our individual contributions to the Cosmos, we acknowledge its wholeness and become holists. To make such a contribution requires an understanding of the cosmic significance of that contribution. When the artist creates a work of art or the scientist devises a new theory, they cannot do so with seeing the wider significance of their contributions which belong to all humanity. When some thing new is brought into being, the Cosmos is enlarged and invigorated. The more we know about humanity, life and the universe, the more we contribute to its content which embraces all human activities. The Cosmos thrives on the activity of our brains in engaging with its contents. It is also vitalised by the additional order, arrangement, symmetry, regularity, system, pattern, and planning we introduce that did not exist before. The act of acquiring knowledge is a form of ordering and arranging material that is brought into and takes its place in the greater corpus of human knowledge. The 'all' is incorporated into the 'one'; the microcosm becomes the macrocosm, and the macrocosm becomes the microcosm. A constant interaction between these outlooks is the basis of all intellectual activity. Thus, holists are the ultimate polymaths or intellectuals who bring all available knowledge together to serve humanity to the best of their abilities.

The Cosmos is therefore a metaphor for all human knowledge, artistic and physical achievements. It metaphorically brings everything together and makes us to think more precisely and productively about the human condition and our contribution to the universe. The more everything is brought together, the more order and rationality there is in the universe. It is the simplest way to include all the products of our intelligence and creativity that have been objectified in any way. If they are out there for example in the internet then they are within the sphere of Cosmos. In our appreciation of the Cosmos, we cannot exclude any field of knowledge that is understood and appreciated by human beings. In the cosmian sphere, the scientist becomes a holistic intellectual and acquires the imagination and breadth of vision worthy of a holistic visionary. The emphasis is therefore on the continuous creativity of humanity.

B. The Meaning of Cosmos

The origin of the word. The word 'Cosmos' is from the Greek, κόσμος, originally meaning 'order' as opposed to disorder or chaos. It was extended to refer to the perfect ordering of the universe. The notion gives us reasons to justify our existence in the universe. In particular, it provides a context within which we can make more sense of our relationship to the universe as a whole. To go into its content in more detail, it contains not only everything of qualitative value that we bring into existence, but also the activity involved in such overarching, unifying notions as the internet, cyberspace, and the sociosphere. It thus includes all our social activities, namely, our communications, information, knowledge, culture, art and all our achievements in technology, business or whatever. Everything of a creative and innovative nature that distinguishes us as a species contributes to the Cosmos, wherein our existence is justified. It therefore includes everything that engages us as intelligent beings and makes more of what we are as unique beings. By these activities we are responsible for the beauty and ordering of the universe that makes for the Cosmos which is more than the material universe that we see around us.

The universe began in a state of infinite order and has tended towards greater disorder through time. The order that we are creating in making sense of the universe's workings contributes however minutely towards the reconstitution of the universe's original order. Our culture generates masses of information that introduces order into the universe that is otherwise losing information as it disintegrates. While the universe moves from order to disorder, life creates negative entropy by introducing order to counter this ugly and disorderly trend. The Cosmos embodies the re-ordering of the universe that only intelligent beings such as ourselves are capable of doing. It represents the increasing order that we and other life-forms bring into the universe which counters the universe's entropic dispersal, though in a very small way. It is our contribution to the far future when the universe may be mastered and its inevitable disintegration countered by beings far more advanced than we are.

The notion of Cosmos is useful in objectifying our activities. By including all aspects of our humanity in the Cosmos, we can better judge their value. For example, we can then think of a stunning painting such as Botticelli's *Venus* or an enchanting piece of music such as Beethoven's *Pastoral Symphony* as somehow going beyond humanity without being anything divine or supernatural. Our feelings are entirely physical and material, however transcendental we may feel them to be. Objects of beauty have a cosmic importance of their own, which is nevertheless entirely human and indicative of ourselves and our achievements. In this way, we can distinguish our cosmic judgments from humanity and its activities without losing the humanity which gave rise to them and which sustains them. In other words, the Cosmos gives us an interactive template by which to judge ourselves without dehumanising and lowering us like the divine perspective tends to do.

We thereby recognise that our achievements are not simply our own but have a permanent effect on the world and the universe at large. What we have done as a species exists as a permanent possibility of access in the future, even if by means at present unknown to us. It is therefore useful to think of everything that we value as being out there permanently available in being contributions to the Cosmos which is the ultimate ordering of a universe that is otherwise becoming increasingly disordered and chaotic.

How the Cosmos amplifies our humanity. We are important because of the new and different things that we do that contribute to the Cosmos. We can make this contribution, for instance, through art and science, that is to say: (1) by our creativity and our beautification of everything around us and (2) by our ordering of things and reasoning about them. Everything we do that is new and creative contributes to the Cosmos. Everything we do that brings order, reason and sense into being also contributes to the Cosmos. It is the ultimate end to which we can contribute by our thoughts and deeds that order and beautify our surroundings in a material way. The mere fact of living means that we are ordering our surroundings by relating ourselves to everything and making everything a part of ourselves. Our lives gain more sense and direction when they are seen as participating in a perpetual quest for greater beauty and order than what existed before. The notion of Cosmos thus provides the context in which we can gauge the value of what we are doing in relation to the whole universe.

In so far as our lives are disorderly, negative and self-destructive they lack cosmic value and significance. Such lives are entirely human and understandable but they arrest our cosmic development. There is no reason why we all cannot be productive and purposeful persons doing our bit to benefit humanity, each in our own way. Everyone is capable of being cosmically competent in that way, and the notion of Cosmos amplifies and illuminates the importance of our contributions however insignificant we may feel them to be. Therefore, it is incumbent on society to help everyone to find their own way of contributing meaningfully to the Cosmos. This is obviously a role for our education system which is performing at present only partially and perfunctorily in face of the infinite possibilities of human accomplishment.

The Cosmos comes into being at the medial area between the very large and the very small where intelligent beings such as ourselves make their original contributions to its content. But in that sense the Cosmos exists only ideally, that is to say, as an ideal that inspires and directs our thinking about the universe, its contents and our relationship to these contents. It is an ideal repository of everything worthwhile that we as individuals and as a species have accomplished. Though it is ideal, it is not imaginary. The fact that we are doing all these things and changing things in external reality is evidence of the objectivity of our achievements and that objectivity is concreted in the notion of Cosmos.

There is no need to believe uncritically in the existence of the Cosmos. It is only postulated as an ideal existent used as an interactive interface between our subjective thinking and the objective universe. It is a useful tool in ascertaining our place in the universe. Believing uncritically in the existence of a god is self-defeating compared with postulating the existence of a Cosmos. It is a human thing that refers to us for our purposes, whereas the notion of a God is an inhuman thing that has often been used for inhuman purposes, such as killing those who refuse to believe in it. Anyone not seeing any use or need for the notion of Cosmos is simply lacking a potentially useful notion and nothing more. It is no more an aspect of our culture such as classical music, rock'n'roll, science fiction, modern art, football or any other aspect that some people follow and other do not. On the other hand, there are educational benefits in taking a cosmic view to understand what it has to offer in helping us to appreciate our place in the universe. Taking a theistic or deistic view means giving up and withdrawing from the cosmic fray wherein lies our future and our destiny.

The Cosmos is our gift to the universe in gratitude for our lives. In this way, we make more of ourselves by making cosmic comparisons. This use of Cosmos amplifies our humanity without being inhuman, divine, or supernatural. Its contents are entirely of our own making and are made into objects that are in a sense our offerings to the universe. They are there to be appreciated and judged by posterity and other intelligent beings. Our gift to the universe is what we are and what we have achieved and this is embodied in the notion of Cosmos. We give the creations and products to the universe via the Cosmos in appreciation for the gift of life which the generation of the universe has made possible.

How the Cosmos unifies our thinking and doing. The notion of the Cosmos is particularly important as a way of unifying the diversity of human thought and activity. No matter how diverse, conflicting and contradictory our thoughts and actions may be, they are all subsumable into the Cosmos. They are unified not by being reduced to each other in a logically deductive manner, but by having their place in the overall mantle of the Cosmos. Thus, the Cosmos functions as an inductive, synthetic notion that interrelates everything by being a higher context within they can be considered in relation to each other.

While our beliefs are humanised within the Cosmos, they are not made any more truthful by that process. All the ideas and beliefs of religion and philosophy may be unified within the Cosmos. But it is not a repository of truths but of human intellectual products. These ideas and beliefs belong there because they are the products of human beings making their mark on the world. But the fact that they are unified therein tells us nothing about their truth or falsity. The Cosmos is their holdall and not their arbiter. They are unified in something that goes beyond them and that makes sense of them in a wider context. They are humanised and made part of our culture as a whole without being judged in terms of evidential or logical truth.

In this way, we can agree about the value of beliefs without agreeing about their truth. The unifying function of the Cosmos helps us to agree among ourselves about things that otherwise seem disparate and irreconcilable. We can agree about the cosmic nature of beliefs and ideas without necessarily agreeing about their truth or falsity. The value of Buddhism as a cultural contribution can be agreed upon without believing in it or regarding its tenets as being true. It is seen to be a valuable contribution to human culture but that does not make it true or false. This distinction ensures that religious beliefs cannot be considered absolute truths since they rank alongside other beliefs within the Cosmos without being pre-eminent among them.

Its unifying aspect can be useful in moving us forward to a better future and in making greater cultural progress. We can better see the limitations and defects of particular beliefs by comparing them within the context of the Cosmos. Some beliefs can be seen to be more culturally valuable than others. For example, the value of Scientology may compare unfavourably with the value of Buddhism. Some aspects of beliefs are valuable because they apply more widely to all humankind and are not just specific to particular belief systems. But making decisions as to truth and falsity must be based on facts and events in the physical world and not on anything whose cultural value must be evaluated on cosmic principles.

C. The Cosmic Contribution of Science

Without a doubt, our scientific knowledge constitutes our best and most important contribution to the Cosmos. It is by far the most useful, the most illuminating, and the most far-reaching of all cosmic contributions. Our increasing medical knowledge is indispensable to the future well-being of the human race, and our increasing scientific understanding of the universe and its contents is needed to ensure our survival as a species. The value of scientific knowledge to our culture is immeasurable. It is invaluable but not exorbitantly so. It has immense qualitative value but that value does not overarch the value of every other aspect of our culture.

As science is only one cosmic contributor among many, this fact determines its limitations. Its role in our culture is more clearly circumscribed when we see that it stands alongside the arts and other human activities in its contributions to the Cosmos. It may eclipse every other human activity in what it can do for us but it is still equal to everything else in relation to the Cosmos. For example, the contributions of art and music are scarcely comparable to those of science. But they have a human value that goes beyond all scientific analysis. They are human activities whose value is inestimable in terms of what they give us from aesthetic and emotional points of view. They are needed by us in our daily lives and they are not to be marginalised as their loss would significantly diminish our quality of life.

Science is not necessarily 'omnicompetent'. Scientific methods are extremely important in enabling us to understand the workings of the material world. But these methods are largely abstract and mathematical and do not apply to qualitative value that is largely subjective, intuitive and holistic. That value cannot be pinned down by mathematical or logical methods which depend on discrete distinctions being made and on wholes being reduced to their parts. Science is not 'omnicompetent' in that it is not competent to fulfil the role of other cosmic contributors which do not fall within the context of science. It is not competent to tell us what human feelings are all about. It is not competent to measure these feelings or reduce them to anything scientifically analysable. Any such attempts would violate our integrity as individuals. Everyone has a right to their own feelings without their being imposed on them by 'scientific' means. As it stands, science cannot explain everything about the universe and it cannot predict the future of our species. It also gives us no clue as to what we are supposed to do with ourselves in the future. In short, there are lots of ways in which science is quite useless to us.

It is not possible to extend the scientific method indefinitely, otherwise art, for instance, would be entirely mechanical and mathematical and the machines could take over. There is a sense in which all aspects of human culture may be subjected to scientific methods of one sort or another. Statistical analysis is one example of this. But they are equally subject to other methods which are not regarded as scientific. From the 1970s onwards, physicists themselves have widened the scope of physics to include not only philosophy in general but also eastern mysticism. Books such as *The Tao of Physics, Wholeness and the Implicate Order, God and the New Physics*, all mark the physicists' loss of confidence in the ability of physics to supply the ultimate answers. But in reality they do not extend the boundaries of science so much as involve a retreat into philosophy and mysticism in search of answers, (as I argue in my book, *What is Philosophy?*)

From a scientific point of view, the Cosmos functions as an interactive process by which we can interact ideally with the reality of the universe to make better sense of it. We arrive at ideas and then test them in relation to external reality. In interacting with the universe through science, and in doing our meaningful and purposeful deeds that add to the order and beauty of the universe, the Cosmos comes into its own as the interface between the stark materiality of the universe and our ideal, subjective thinking about the universe and its contents. It reflects our intermediary position between its vastness and minisculeness. Thus, on the one hand, the Cosmos resides between the macro-universe of astrophysics and the micro-universe of quantum physics. On the other hand, it is placed between our ideal musings and the stark reality of physical existence. Ideality refers to our subjective thoughts and speculations that we constantly relate to reality to arrive at a realistic view of ourselves and the universe. The Cosmos grows and develops as a result of such interactions. For example, as our understanding of quantum physics increasingly approximates the realities of the universe, the Cosmos grows accordingly. The following diagram brings these four relationships together to symbolise their contributions to the Cosmos which is centred between them.

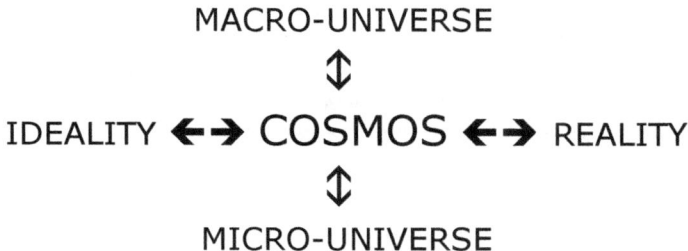

MACRO-UNIVERSE
$\updownarrow$

IDEALITY $\leftrightarrow$ COSMOS $\leftrightarrow$ REALITY
$\updownarrow$

MICRO-UNIVERSE

An Interactive Cosmic Quadrifoil Matrix

The above quadrifoil matrix shows how cosmic activity progresses interactively. It depicts the four dimensions of interactivity that are necessary and sufficient for the progress of cosmic activity. The Cosmos in the middle capitalises on our interactive efforts to reconcile the macro-universe with the micro-universe. We do so by constantly relating ideality to reality and *vice versa*. This enables us to put scientific activity into a wider context beyond that of explaining the nitty gritty of how the universe works in concrete mathematical terms. It puts that activity in the context of human activity in general and shows its Cosmic importance.

The diagram also shows that the Cosmos results from the interaction between the physical reality of the universe and the ideal world that we create in thinking about anything, real or unreal. It assumes that the universe's reality comprises only the material and physical parts of the Cosmos. This assumption would presumably be accepted by materialists who deny the existence of anything beyond the material universe. However, sceptics and idealists may deny even that assumption but in so doing they risk disconnecting their thinking from external reality altogether. Thus, the Cosmos reflects the fact that we stay in touch with reality by constantly interacting with it to ensure that our ideas accurately represent reality as far as humanly possible. In short, the diagram depicts dualist interaction which is elaborated in more detail in my book entitled *The Promise of Dualism.*

D. The Cosmic Significance of Past Religions

The real cosmic value of religion. All the religions of the past have made their respective contributions to the Cosmos. The study of these contributions is an intimate part of cosmic research since they all have something to say about the human condition and about what it is to be human. But this is only when we consider them historically. Their cosmic value is lost when they are considered as active vehicles of truth that are set against other religions and sources of religious thought and feeling. Their cosmic significance depends on their no longer being proselytising religions whose truths are forced on people in an exclusive way that brooks no deviation from these truths. Thus, Cosmos is inclusive of all religions that are not themselves exclusive.

Religious writings make their own cosmic contribution and they include all the sacred works of all the religions of the world, most notably such documents as the Bible, the Talmud, the Koran, Buddhist scriptures, the Upanishads, and the Bhagavad Gita. The range of writings to be included under this heading can be seen in works such as Bouquet's *The Sacred Books of the World.* This book includes writings as diverse as Sumerian Prayers, Homeric Hymns, Zoroastrian Literature, and Japanese Shinto Literature. We can add to this list our growing understanding of ancient religious writings such as those of the ancient Egyptians and Mayans. All these writings are important to our understanding of how human religious thought developed, and of how diverse that thought is. Although humanist thinking has transcended religious thought, the study of the latter helps us to understand the past trains of thought by which we have arrived at a more advanced understanding of our plight and place in the universe.

The Cosmos as a successor to the comparative religion movement. Within the context of the Cosmos, all religions are brought together eclectically with the hope of convergence at some date in the future. This unifying procedure contrasts strongly with the eclecticism and syncretism of past attempts to bring them together. Comparative religion is an example of an attempt to unify all religions by giving an account of them in a loose and eclectic fashion. No religion is treated as being better than any other though an attempt is made to pinpoint their common features. The comparative religion movement failed because it had no method or system of thought by which all the incompatible religions could be brought together into a unity. The notion of Cosmos is step towards providing such a method of unifying religious thought and practice. It provides a framework within which all religious views and sentiments can be accommodated without necessarily being antithetical to each other.

Religious prophets are those people who have seen beyond the material world and have emphasised the importance of our cosmic musings about our existence. In a sense, we are all cosmic prophets who have views about the cosmic nature of the universe and who strive to communicate these views to other people. Compared the well-known prophets, most of us have made fairly modest contributions to the cosmic content. The most important of all the cosmic prophets who have walked the face of the Earth are those who have had the most impact on the history of the human race. They introduced new religions and thereby changed the thinking of humankind by these acts. The most important of all cosmic prophets include Akhenaton, Moses, Zoroaster, Buddha, Confucius, Jesus Christ and Mohammed. Whether the effects of these prophets have been altogether to the good of humankind is entirely another matter. The notion of Cosmos now gives us the opportunity to establish the real and lasting importance of these figures. We do so by accounting for their influence on their contemporaries, disciples, and followers. The facts about them can be studied objectively so that their true value to humanity can be established beyond doubt.

Religious truths contribute to the Cosmos in so far as they add to our understanding of the human condition. For instance, the distinctive advances of the Christian message contained in the Sermon of the Mount are permanent contributions to the Cosmos. We ought to be *Christians* in our attitude towards our potential enemies and in our attempts to understand people rather than hate them. Equally, we ought to be *Jews* in our respect for family life; *Muslims* in our respect for authority and absolute values; *Buddhists* in our use of meditation to reach our inner being; *Hindus* in our appreciation of spirituality; and so on. In this way, we can make use of the strengths and truths in particular religions without believing in the unbelievable and without practising senseless, superfluous rituals. Such cosmic ideals were anticipated by the comparative religion movement which has its roots in the religious toleration established in Great Britain after the Civil War of the 17th century. In understanding the merits of other religions, we have the possibility of transcending them all within the context of the Cosmos. Also, by taking account of all religions and respecting their respective contributions, we pass on to posterity what is worthwhile about them.

It is therefore clear that the traditional religions have no future as self-sufficient, mutually antagonistic movements. By themselves, they no longer take us anywhere as they have become too ingrown and limited in their outlook and lack competent answers to the human predicament. The exclusivity of these religions means that they exclude unbelievers and heretics. The four great prophets of religion – Moses, Jesus, Buddha and Mohammed – got it wrong, each in their different ways. The first and last of them made far too much of a non-existent entity with the aim of belittling people unjustifiably and boosting their power over them without limit. Jesus made too much of unworldliness and meekness. The Buddha made too much of introspective meditation to the point of vacuity. Moreover, they all failed to see the bigger picture. Their view of human potential was also limited by the state of human knowledge available to them in their respective lifetimes.

To summarise, the Cosmos is ourselves writ large. It is a way of thinking about our accomplishments in the abstract. In being all-inclusive concept, it compares favourably with exclusivity of religion, which typically excludes unbelievers and heretics. There is no need to believe implicitly in the existence of the Cosmos as it is only a means of making sense of humanity's contributions to the universe. It is enough to see its usefulness in that regard and then to dispense with it. There is no point in opposing it as it is only a harmless abstraction that does not require anything of anyone. Its role is entirely descriptive and there is nothing prescriptive about it. If it does nothing for you, it is nothing to you. Yet it is a way of describing everything about humanity and of our achievements. It becomes highly meaningful and useful in that context, as it is a holistic aid by which we can see ourselves as an invaluable part of the whole and thus add meaning and purpose to our lives.

Afterword

The holist view is about doing worthwhile things by looking at the whole picture. True belief consists in serving humanity. Any other kind of belief does humanity a disservice in so far as it lessens and debases it. It is more important to have a justifiable faith in ourselves than an unjustifiable faith in some non-existent entity that is beyond our ken. Unless we are constantly justifying our existence by doing the best we can, we are existing and not living. Life is not meant to be easy and it is better to make it difficult for ourselves for the best possible reasons and not just do things because we want to feel better.

Too many people are too much into themselves nowadays. Self-obsession and self-centredness has become the norm. The whole picture is neglected in favour of immediacies. Many minds are full of mindfulness but empty of purpose. In the face of such inwardness, this book aims to take people out of themselves by emphasising the bigger picture and showing the benefits of looking at things as a whole.

We are supposed to humble ourselves before God but that takes us back into ourselves as the idea of God is essentially subjective; everyone can have their own idea of it. It has impeded our progress in many ways as no agreement can be reached about what it is. God is a perennial source of divisiveness and hostility; it is a disuniting entity that sets us against each other. It is no more than a figment of our imagination – a big daddy in the sky or a Nobodaddy as the poet William Blake disparagingly called it. There is no future in God, and it's time to move on and take responsibility for ourselves and the universe. Our knowledge of latter is growing by the day and it gives us a very clear view of our cosmic insignificance. We no longer need God to cower before or pretend arrogantly that we are made in its image. We now have to work on our own image which is ugly enough from many perspectives.

A better approach is to be clearer about our place in the universe so that we make neither too little nor too much of ourselves by being stuck in one extreme or the other. This is possible by taking the holistic view offered in this book. By taking account of ourselves as a whole we can see better what our lives are really all about. We can be as large or small, as important or unimportant as we presume ourselves to be. By oscillating between these extremes we can move forward into a better future instead of being stuck in the logjam of the past. This book is therefore an example of the dualist point of view that I have already outlined in my book, *The Promise of Dualism*.

But the dualist view is not enough if it leaves us stranded in the middle of things without a definite way forward. Logic and reason are also not enough. They can mislead us with dogmatic certainties, like the bankers and market makers who regard their algorithms as sacrosanct until complex realities prove them to be over-simplified and unreliable. We need to develop our intuitions so that we arrive at reliable certainties and make the right decisions. Our emotions can get the better of us when we are inwardly underdeveloped. We need layers of self-knowledge to gain control of our self-destructive impulses and to protect us against ourselves. This requires us to build up our inner being which is the source of intuition and this is the great gift that the holistic view can give us. We learn to think about things from the broadest and widest perspective and are more inclined to do the right thing by ourselves, by everyone and for the benefit of life in general. Thus, the holistic view outlined in this book is at least part of the answer concerning what the human condition is all about and what we can do to improve it and make it fit for the purposes of futurity.

www.ingramcontent.com/pod-product-compliance
Lightning Source LLC
Chambersburg PA
CBHW070536030426
42337CB00016B/2226